GW00372029

Marguerite Duras

MANCHESTER
UNIVERSITY PRESS

FRENCH FILM DIRECTORS

DIANA HOLMES and ROBERT INGRAM *series editors*
DUDLEY ANDREW *series consultant*

Jean-Jacques Beineix   PHIL POWRIE

Luc Besson   SUSAN HAYWARD

Bertrand Blier   SUE HARRIS

Robert Bresson   KEITH READER

Claude Chabrol   GUY AUSTIN

Diane Kurys   CARRIE TARR

Georges Méliès   ELIZABETH EZRA

Jean Renoir   MARTIN O'SHAUGHNESSY

Coline Serreau   BRIGITTE ROLLET

François Truffaut   DIANA HOLMES AND ROBERT INGRAM

Agnès Varda   ALISON SMITH

FRENCH FILM DIRECTORS

Marguerite Duras

RENATE GÜNTHER

Manchester University Press
MANCHESTER AND NEW YORK

distributed exclusively in the USA by Palgrave

The right of Renate Günther to be identified as the author of this work has
been asserted by her in accordance with the Copyright, Designs and Patents
Act 1988.

Published by Manchester University Press
Oxford Road, Manchester M13 9NR, UK
and Room 400, 175 Fifth Avenue, New York, NY 10010, USA
www.manchesteruniversitypress.co.uk

Distributed exclusively in the USA by
Palgrave, 175 Fifth Avenue, New York,
NY 10010, USA

Distributed exclusively in Canada by
UBC Press, University of British Columbia, 2029 West Mall,
Vancouver, BC, Canada V6T 1Z2

British Library Cataloguing-in-Publication Data
A catalogue record for this book is available from the British Library

Library of Congress Cataloging-in-Publication Data applied for

ISBN 0 7190 5756 6 *hardback*
    0 7190 5757 4 *paperback*

First published 2002

10 09 08 07 06 05 04 03 02   10 9 8 7 6 5 4 3 2 1

Typeset in Scala with Meta display
by Koinonia, Manchester
Printed in Great Britain
by Bookcraft (Bath) Ltd, Midsomer Norton

Für Mama und zur Erinnerung an Pappa

Für Mama und zur Erinnerung an Pappa.

Contents

List of plates

All photos are reproduced with permission by Jean Mascolo.
All courtesy of BFI Stills, Posters and Designs.

Series editors' foreword

To an anglophone audience, the combination of the words 'French' and 'cinema' evokes a particular kind of film: elegant and wordy, sexy but serious – an image as dependent on national stereotypes as is that of the crudely commercial Hollywood blockbuster, which is not to say that either image is without foundation. Over the past two decades, this generalised sense of a significant relationship between French identity and film has been explored in scholarly books and articles, and has entered the curriculum at university level and, in Britain, at A level. The study of film as an art-form and (to a lesser extent) as industry, has become a popular and widespread element of French Studies, and French cinema has acquired an important place within Film Studies. Meanwhile, the growth in multi-screen and 'art-house' cinemas, together with the development of the video industry, has led to the greater availability of foreign-language films to an English-speaking audience. Responding to these developments, this series is designed for students and teachers seeking information and accessible but rigorous critical study of French cinema, and for the enthusiastic filmgoer who wants to know more.

The adoption of a director-based approach raises questions about *auteurism*. A series that categorises films not according to period or to genre (for example), but to the person who directed them, runs the risk of espousing a romantic view of film as the product of solitary inspiration. On this model, the critic's role might seem to be that of discovering continuities, revealing a necessarily coherent set of themes and motifs which correspond to the particular genius of the individual. This is not our aim: the *auteur* perspective on film, itself most clearly articulated in France in the early 1950s, will be interrogated in certain volumes of the series, and, throughout, the director will be treated as one highly significant element in a complex process of film production and reception which includes socio-economic and political determinants, the work of a large and highly skilled team of artists and technicians, the mechanisms of production and distribution, and the complex and multiply determined responses of spectators.

The work of some of the directors in the series is already known outside France, that of others is less so – the aim is both to provide informative and original English-language studies of established figures, and to extend the range of French directors known to anglophone students of cinema. We intend the series to contribute to the promotion of the informal and formal study of French films, and to the pleasure of those who watch them.

DIANA HOLMES
ROBERT INGRAM

Acknowledgements

My thanks go to Madeleine Borgomano, Christiane Blot-Labarrère, Owen Heathcote and Michelle Royer who helped me locate some of the material used in this book and to Guy Austin and Geraldine Walsh-Harrington for their advice and support. I am grateful to the British Academy for the grant that enabled me to carry out the research for this book and to Jean Mascolo for his permission to reproduce the photographs. I would also like to thank Barbara Lambert whose vision guided my research in Paris and Beryl Rayner whose kindness and encouragement have been greatly appreciated. Finally, a special thank-you to Cath for her many helpful suggestions and her support throughout this project.

Acknowledgements

1

Autobiography, history and politics

When she embarked on a second career as a film director in the late 1960s, Marguerite Duras was already a well-known and highly acclaimed novelist and playwright who had published fourteen literary texts since her first novel *Les Impudents* (1943). What binds her fictional texts and her films together is that both are inhabited by the people, places and events of her life, as she remarked in an interview with Michelle Porte: 'One is haunted by one's lived experience, one must let it have its way' (Porte 1983: 61). Although Duras transformed her experience into art, she did not do so by simply telling the 'story of her life', as she did not believe that the chaos of memory could or should be subjugated to the contrived order of a linear and logically structured novelistic or filmic narrative. Instead, she isolated significant moments in her life and condensed them, in fictionalised form, into the recurring scenarios that run through her texts and her films. This repetition with variations of the same core material is one of the hallmarks of Duras's work, as she creates clusters of references through which texts and films both mirror and transform one another. But what makes her art so compelling is the fact that she universalised her particular world by emptying its people and places of their individual identities, enabling readers and spectators alike to project their own stories, thoughts and fantasies on to the bare outlines offered. If Duras's creative enterprise was shaped to a large extent by memories of her childhood and adolescence, her involvement in the political history of France since the Second World War played an equally important role, particularly in her cinema. Indeed, a number of her films made in the 1970s were directly inspired by political developments which characterised contemporary French society. Bearing in mind this dual influence, the sections that follow will present an outline of Duras's early life and of her later political preoccupations, highlighting the relationship between these two dimensions and her films.

Vietnam: the cinema of childhood

Marguerite Donnadieu (Duras was her pen name) was born on 4 April 1914 in Gia-Dinh on the outskirts of Saigon in Vietnam, which was then part of the French colony of Indochina. The only girl in the Donnadieu family, Marguerite had two older brothers, Pierre and Paul, as well as two stepbrothers from her father's first marriage. Her parents were both teachers who had emigrated from France to Indochina, attracted by the propaganda disseminated by the French state which promised its citizens glorious opportunities and an opulent lifestyle in the colonies. Initially the family's expectations were met, as Emile Donnadieu's work as a teacher of mathematics allowed them to live in various sumptuous colonial residences, among others a former royal palace at Phnom-Penh in Cambodia. However, due to severe illness, the father was obliged to return to France where he bought the property of 'le Platier' near the village of Duras in the Périgord region of south-west France. He died there in 1921 when Marguerite was only 7 years old. The pseudonym 'Duras' evidently has its origin in this part of France and was chosen, perhaps not so much for its paternal connotations as for its childhood associations, as Marie Donnadieu and her three children went to live there for two years before returning to Indochina in 1924. Because of her father's absence during much of her childhood, her memories of him were fairly vague and certainly not as powerful as those of her mother who, after the father's death, became the absolute focal point of the Donnadieu family. Whether we look at Duras's autobiographical writings or her fictional texts, the father appears at best as a marginal or, occasionally, as a tragic character, such as that of the old man in the 1962 novel *L'Après-midi de Monsieur Andesmas*. Similarly, in her films the paternal figure is largely absent, except in the *Aurélia Steiner* (1979) sequence where he acquires a new and unexpected significance. Overall, however, it is clear that Duras's filmic imagination is firmly located within a female universe, centred around her evocations of the maternal and the feminine.

Following the father's death, the Donnadieu family were forced to abandon their previously affluent existence, plummeting into a life of destitution and hardship, as the mother tried to scrape a meagre living on her widow's pension and the small salary she received for teaching French to Vietnamese children in an indigenous school. The family were also marginalised by the white colonial bourgeoisie who categorised them as part of an underclass in their social hierarchy. It was in this context of poverty and social exclusion that the cinema first made its impact on the life of the young Duras. Seeing herself as an outsider, different from the other white girls in the colony, she found refuge in the Eden Cinema in Saigon, where she felt particularly enthralled by silent movies starring Charlie Chaplin. It is interesting to note here certain similarities between Duras and Truffaut, for whom the cinema also provided temporary respite from the problems and difficulties of childhood.[1] For Duras, cinema also represented a place where social barriers and inequalities dissolved into the darkness of the auditorium, described in her 1950 novel *Un barrage contre le Pacifique* as 'la nuit artificielle et démocratique du cinéma'[2] (Duras 1950: 188). This novel recounts a disastrous episode in her early life when, in 1924, her mother used every penny of her savings to buy a piece of land near the sea at Prey-Nop in Cambodia. The land soon proved to be useless, as every summer the ricefields she had planted there were invaded and destroyed by the tides of the Pacific Ocean. Determined not to be beaten by the colonial administrators, who had deliberately cheated her and were now threatening to repossess the land, Marie Donnadieu enlisted the help of her Vietnamese neighbours to build a massive dam against the sea. However, this sea wall which they had taken six months to build was also ruined, as the wood from which it was made was eaten away by thousands of crabs. Subsequently, the family were forced to leave Cambodia and returned to Saigon where the mother suffered a severe nervous breakdown.

Duras's relationship with and memories of her mother were marked by a profound ambivalence. In some of her autobiographical writings, she spoke with tenderness and admiration about this power-

1 For a fuller discussion of this aspect of Truffaut's early life, see Holmes and Ingram (1998): 13.
2 'the artificial and democratic night of the cinema'

ful and determined woman to whom, she said, she owed everything. She described her generosity and portrayed her as a memorable literary figure, comical, outrageous and adored by her children: 'Tous les trois nous étions fous de notre mère, et nous avons dû la rendre heureuse'[3] (Duras 1993: 199). On the other hand, however, she suffered immensely, throughout most of her life, as a result of her mother's rejection of and physical violence towards her (Duras 1993: 204). Despite the mother's protestations to the contrary, it was clear to Duras that she had always preferred her eldest son to the two younger children. In the essay 'Mothers' she draws a harrowing picture, either real or imaginary, of her mother who, on her deathbed, asked to see only her favourite son: 'Elle n'a réclamé qu'une seule présence, celle de ce fils. J'étais dans la chambre, je les ai vus s'embrasser en pleurant, désespérés de se séparer. Ils ne m'ont pas vue'[4] (Duras 1993: 197). Although she was a teacher, the mother took little interest in art or literature and fiercely resented her daughter's literary success, convinced that she would have had a better career in business. When Duras presented her with a copy of *Un barrage contre le Pacifique*, written in homage to her mother, the latter strongly disapproved both of the book and of its author. Bearing in mind these biographical indications, it is reasonable to conjecture that the work of Duras expresses a desire to return to her ideal of the early mother/child relationship, where an imaginary sense of union would prevail over separation and conflict. In this respect, Madeleine Borgomano has rightly argued that the cinema of Duras functions both as a substitute for the mother and as a return to her origins (Borgomano 1985: 25). While I would agree that Duras's films do replace the mother, I would also suggest that they reinscribe the maternal through a displacement of unrequited love for the mother on to the figure of Anne-Marie Stretter, the mythical heroine of Duras's most acclaimed film *India Song* (1975).

This female protagonist plays such a crucial role in the work of Duras that it is worth examining her origins in Duras's childhood and the reasons for her prominence in some of the novels and films of the 1960s and 1970s. Anne-Marie Stretter is a composite fictional construct inspired by Elisabeth Striedter, a wealthy woman of Swiss

3 'All three of us were crazy about our mother, and we must have made her happy.'
4 'She only asked for one person to be present, her son. I was in the room, I saw them hugging and crying, desperate because they had to leave each other. They didn't see me.'

origin, whose husband was the general administrator of the province of Chau Doc in Indochina. In the 1920s the Striedters moved to Vinh-Long on the Mekong river, where the Donnadieus were also living at that time. It was here that the young Marguerite first saw Elisabeth Striedter, as she passed by in her black chauffeur-driven limousine. The girl was stunned and overwhelmed by this woman's beauty, elegance and unobtrusiveness, providing a fantasised escape from her own family's poverty and the disappointing relationship with her mother. This, combined with the fact that Elisabeth Striedter had two daughters, roughly the same age as Marguerite, made her the desired maternal and feminine model. In *Les Lieux de Marguerite Duras* she wrote: 'Je pense que c'était ça, elle, Anne-Marie Stretter, le modèle parental pour moi, le modèle maternel, ou plutôt le modèle féminin'[5] (Duras and Porte 1977: 65). It is interesting to note here that, in this comment, Duras uses the name of her own fictional character, suggesting that for her the real and the imaginary woman became interchangeable. This blurring of fact and fiction is also apparent in Duras's elaboration of an episode which occurred shortly after Elisabeth Striedter's arrival in Vinh-Long when a young man committed suicide out of love for her (Duras and Porte 1977: 64–5). Marguerite, profoundly affected by this incident, interpreted it as evidence of the conjunction of desire and death which, condensed in the figure of Anne-Marie Stretter, was to become a constant element in both her written texts and her films. But Anne-Marie Stretter represented more than a maternal model or a mirror of feminine identity, although both these aspects are undoubtedly present in the fictional and filmic constructions of her. The powerful impact she had on Duras, combined with her very elusiveness and inaccessibility, transformed her into the ideal object of desire, providing a driving force that inspired her work over a period of at least ten years. Commenting on the role of Anne-Marie Stretter in *India Song* she said: 'What is played out as drama there is my fascination, the love I bear her. I wonder if that love hasn't always existed' (Porte 1983: 55–6). I would conclude from this that, through Anne-Marie Stretter, Durassian cinema reveals a paradoxical dual process, aligning the sometimes deadly desire for regression to the maternal with desire as a progressive and creative force, clearly evident in the radical innovations of *India Song*.

5 'I think that's what Anne-Marie Stretter was for me, the parental model, the maternal or rather the feminine model.'

Anne-Marie Stretter first entered Duras's fictional universe in 1964, when she briefly appeared in the novel *Le Ravissement de Lol V. Stein*. She occupied centre stage in the 1965 novel *Le Vice-consul* along with the eponymous male character. Key aspects from both novels in terms of narrative and protagonists were then incorporated into *India Song*, so that, at a diegetic level, the film is to some extent a composite of the written texts which preceded it. However, one crucial difference is that, whereas in *Le Vice-consul* the heroine's death is only briefly implied in the novel's conclusion, in *India Song* there is a much stronger suggestion that she commits suicide by drowning. It seems that Duras was so deeply affected by Anne-Marie Stretter that her death at the end of the film was the only means by which she could exorcise her own desire for her. As she said in *Marguerite Duras à Montréal*: 'Je vivais une sorte d'amour fou pour cette femme, et je recommençais toujours le même film, toujours le même livre et je me suis dit: "*Il faut qu'elle meure.*" Voilà. Parce qu'elle m'a tellement atteinte'[6] (Lamy and Roy 1981: 33). After a ten-year period of absence, Anne-Marie Stretter made a brief reappearance in the prize-winning 1984 novel *L'Amant*, where Duras's evocation of her clearly lacks its previous intensity.

India Song and the film *Agatha et les lectures illimitées*, made in 1981, resemble each other in so far as both deal with desire that transgresses dominant social codes and practices. *Agatha* revolves around the implicitly incestuous love between brother and sister which, from a biographical perspective, can be seen as a fictional projection of Duras's relationship with her own brother and which echoes the incestuous overtones of her early novels *La Vie tranquille* and *Un Barrage contre le Pacifique*. In her autobiographical writings, Duras affectionately refers to her brother Paul as 'the little brother' – although he was three years older than her – and describes him as her closest friend and the companion with whom she shared her childhood experiences, be it their adventures in the Vietnamese jungle, where Paul allegedly hunted tigers and black panthers, or their complicity when faced with the mother's and the elder brother's tyranny (Duras 1984: 74; 13–14). In her novels and in her cinema Duras highlights above all the emotional intensity of the bond between

6 'I was madly in love with this woman, and I kept making the same films, the same books and I said to myself: "*She has to die.*" That's it. Because she touched me so deeply.'

brother and sister, the impossibility of this 'forbidden love' and the subsequent need for separation. Given her brother's enormous importance in her childhood, Duras was so distraught by his death in 1943 that she herself wanted to die (Duras 1984: 128–9). The brother/sister relationship punctuates her work from the 1940s to the early 1990s, underlining the extent to which she was preoccupied by this part of her early life, in the same way as she remained obsessed by the memory of her mother and of Anne-Marie Stretter.

Another significant figure which reappears in both novels and films is that of the beggarwoman, whose fictional story seems to be based on two separate incidents in Duras's childhood: the first concerns a young Vietnamese woman, who handed her half-dead 2-year-old girl over to Marie Donnadieu, as she was too ill herself to look after the child. From a historical perspective, it is true that many Vietnamese women, who endured extreme poverty, were forced to sell their children to white families. The little girl, who was cared for by Marguerite, died a few days later (Lebelley 1994: 25). In a second episode, recalled in *L'Amant*, Duras talks about an incident where one night she was chased down a dark, deserted street in Vinh-Long by a screaming beggarwoman known as 'la folle de Vinhlong'[7] (Duras 1984: 103). For the terrified Marguerite this tall, emaciated woman came to epitomise her fear of madness which haunted her for most of her life. In her fiction and films she amalgamated the two beggarwomen into one figure, who became one of the central characters in *Le Vice-consul* where her story is told by the writer Peter Morgan. In his narrative the beggarwoman is a 17-year-old girl from Savannakhet in Laos who, because she is pregnant, has been chased from her home and family by her mother. Morgan's fictional account subsequently traces her journey, as she walks a distance of two thousand miles from Savannakhet to Calcutta, where her story joins that of Anne-Marie Stretter and the Vice-Consul of Lahore. It is this version of the beggarwoman that is transposed on to *India Song* and its 1976 sequel *Son nom de Venise dans Calcutta désert*.

The story of the beggarwoman represents not only a part of Duras's personal experience, but also an allegory of the scandal of French colonialism in Indochina, which she witnessed during her childhood. In *Les Parleuses*, for instance, she talks about the exploitation

7 'the madwoman of Vinhlong'

and horrific tortures that the Vietnamese people endured at the hands of their colonisers. Herself excluded from white colonial society, Duras spent her childhood in the company of Vietnamese rather than French children. She grew up bilingual and passed her *baccalauréat* exams in both languages. On the other hand, despite their low social status, the Donnadieus did, of course, still belong to the dominant class, as the mother not only employed Vietnamese servants but also firmly believed in her 'civilising mission', teaching French to Vietnamese children. Despite the resulting ambiguity in Duras's early identity, her later experiences in France and her work are shaped by a strong awareness of and revolt against social and political injustice.

France: a cinema against all ideologies

In 1932, at the age of 18, Duras left Indochina for France, never to return to her country of origin. After a brief visit to the Duras region, she went to Paris to study mathematics, probably under pressure from her mother, but soon abandoned this subject and instead took a degree in law and political science. In 1939, shortly before the outbreak of the Second World War, she married fellow law student Robert Antelme. During the war itself and throughout the German occupation of France, her personal history was somewhat ambiguous which, in the eyes of some of her biographers, puts into question her retrospective self-image as a heroine of the French Resistance. This ambiguity came about because, from 1942 until 1943, Duras occupied the post of secretary at the *commission de contrôle du papier*, a commission set up by the Vichy Government and which was responsible for reading and censoring manuscripts. Duras's particular task was to allocate the paper on which the approved manuscripts were to be printed. This has led Laure Adler, in her recent controversial biography, to imply that Duras was guilty of tacit collaboration (Adler 1998: 159). Considering the extreme circumstances of life in occupied France, I would be more inclined to agree with David Coward's comment that 'Duras was no more a collaborator than publishers who were forced to observe German restrictions, or writers like Sartre who staged plays with official approval' (Coward 1999: 7). In September 1943, together with her husband, she became an active member of the Resistance, working closely with François Mitterrand who saved her life by rescuing her from the Gestapo (Duras and Mitterrand 1986: 34). In 1944, in the same year as Duras's first major novel *La Vie tranquille* was published, Robert Antelme was arrested and deported to Dachau concentration camp, where he was found and brought back to France by Mitterrand shortly after the Liberation in 1945.[8] It was only after her husband's return that Duras learned the true extent of the horrors of the concentration camps, where many of her Jewish friends had died. The shock of this discovery remained with her throughout her life and resulted in her increasing preoccupation with Judaism and the theme of Jewish identity in her work: 'Il y a Auschwitz, toute ma vie, oui, je le porte, rien à faire. C'est là tout le temps'[9] (Lebelley 1994: 136). The holocaust and Jewish exile are major concerns in the 1979 films *Aurélia Steiner, dit Aurélia Melbourne* and *Aurélia Steiner, dit Aurélia Vancouver*, in which Duras attempts to preserve the memory of those who died at Auschwitz and to imagine the effects of the Holocaust, even today, on their descendants.

As a direct result of her experience during the occupation and her friendship with Communist members of the Resistance, such as Edgar Morin and Jean-Francis Rolland, Duras joined the Parti communiste français (PCF) in 1944. From the outset, and although she remained an enthusiastic activist within the party, she was opposed to its cultural politics and the doctrine of socialist realism, according to which writers had to subordinate their ideas and aesthetic concerns to the Leninist view that all art must reflect the Marxist theory of history as class struggle. Writers like Gide, Sartre and Camus, for instance, were condemned as *petit bourgeois* by the party. During her early years in the PCF Duras herself concealed the fact that she was a writer for fear of being denounced as a traitor. She also later recalled that she and other members were under constant surveillance and that any departures from the required codes of conduct were immediately reported (Duras 1977: 120). This extreme authoritarianism, coupled with news of the Stalinist show trials which were taking place in Eastern Europe in 1949, precipitated Duras's growing detachment from the party. Unable to accept the latter's continued loyalty to Stalinism, she finally resigned in 1950 and was then officially expelled

8 Duras gives a harrowing account of the subsequent weeks and months; see Duras, 1985.

9 'There is Auschwitz, all my life, yes, I carry it with me. There's nothing I can do. It's there all the time.'

and labelled as a 'deviationist'. Following this episode, she fiercely denounced the PCF for its slavish adherence to the dictates of the Soviet leadership. In her view, this political dependence was particularly apparent during the events of May 1968, when the party attempted to undermine a revolution that had not been imported from the Soviet Union (Duras 1977: 113–14). For Duras, the utopian ideals of the May movement, with its colourful diversity, could not be slotted into the rigid Marxist frameworks, for such models, limited to the idea of class oppression, would exclude the new liberation movements that emerged from May '68, for example the gay rights and the feminist movements. In the 1980s, furthermore, the PCF defended the Soviet invasion of Afghanistan and subsequently failed to support the Polish workers on strike at the Gdansk shipyard. Duras's fervent anti-PCF stance was closely allied to her commitment to fight all forms of injustice and oppression, including French colonialism in Algeria, the authoritarian structures of Gaullist France and, in the 1970s, the oppression of women.

In 1955, a year after the outbreak of the Algerian War of Independence, Duras and her associates founded the Comité des intellectuels contre la poursuite de la Guerre d'Algérie, a group of left-wing intellectuals who argued for Algerian independence from French rule and was part of a wider anti-colonial movement. The group protested against the torture of Algerian prisoners of war and the atrocities committed by the French army against the civilian population in Algeria. Duras herself hid members of the banned Front de libération nationale (FLN) in her Paris flat. In 1960 she was one of the signatories of the famous *Manifeste des 121*, a statement signed by 121 prominent intellectuels, insisting on the right of French soldiers to desert from their posts in Algeria and asking all French citizens to declare their solidarity with the Algerians, including the immigrant population living in France. Between 1958 and 1962 articles by Duras which were published in *France Observateur* attest to her concern about the links between French colonialism in Algeria and the daily incidents of racism that occurred in France itself, ranging from police harassment of immigrants to racist attacks and murders. Given Duras's personal history, her strong reaction against racism in this context may well have been triggered by her earlier experience of colonial oppression in Indochina and the unimaginable tortures to which the indigenous people were subjected by the French authorities (Duras and Gauthier 1974:

137–8). In Duras's cinema the thematics of colonialism and racism is implicit, for example in the decadent setting of *India Song* and the audible presence of the beggarwoman on the soundtracks of both *India Song* and *Son Nom de Venise dans Calcutta désert*. Similarly, the image-track of the short film *Les Mains négatives* (1979) creates an implicit link between colonialism and the exclusion and exploitation of immigrant workers in contemporary France.

From the late 1950s, Duras was also a staunch opponent of President de Gaulle whose nationalist ideology she saw as a new form of Fascism, not unlike that propagated by General Pétain during the Second World War. Therefore, when de Gaulle returned to power in May 1958, Duras became a founding member of and subsequently the only woman contributor to the anti-Gaullist journal *Le 14 juillet*. This early period of her appearance on the French political scene highlights certain key elements of her political position which are consistently reflected both in the subject matter and the formal structures of her films: her rejection of power and hierarchies, her conviction that the political is also personal and that any social revolution must be built on a radical transformation of the individual subject.

For Duras, the essence of this vision seemed to be distilled in the events of May '68 which promised to unleash an unprecedented revolution in French society. If her political activities had previously revolved around her opposition to the authoritarian structures of Gaullist France, her involvement in May '68 reflects her disillusionment with all ideologies, whether on the left or on the right of the political spectrum. The anarchic spontaneity of the May movement, its refusal of hierarchies and the politicisation of lived experience were all congruous with Duras's own philosophy. Significantly, this period inaugurated her work as a director, as she made her first film *Détruire dit-elle* in 1969. The film is based on a text with the same title which was directly inspired by the events of May '68. In both text and film Duras aims to break down the categories, boundaries and power structures of Western cultures. This process of destruction works partly on the creative level, as the conventional division between text and film becomes blurred. At the same time, Duras demolishes the social hierarchies of pre-1968 society and suggests a utopian communist future as an alternative. As the title of this film suggests, Duras saw May '68 as a period of destruction and transition, during which all existing social formations would necessarily collapse, paving the way towards a more egalitarian world. During the upheavals of the May movement, Duras and some of her friends founded the Comité d'action écrivains–étudiants, a group in which students and writers were to discuss the implications of these events, particularly in relation to the Western constructs of 'the individual' and 'the self'. Duras had always considered the idea of a 'self' as a solid, unified and permanent entity as a potentially oppressive concept, since it limits the expression of contradictions and obstructs any possibility of change. Moreover, for Duras, the construction of rigidly defined identities, whether personal or collective, always entails the exclusion of anyone who is perceived as 'other' in relation to dominant notions of 'self', and hence the creation of social barriers and hierarchical modes of interaction. This is clearly evident in *Détruire dit-elle* where the figure of Bernard Alione becomes an exaggerated, almost caricatural, embodiment of this view of 'self' which can only survive at the expense of the 'other', in this case Bernard's wife Elisabeth and the three Jews. In political terms, there-fore, the film denounces all constructions of identity which can only be maintained through the oppression of others, whether on the basis of sex, nationality, religion or other perceived categories. Hence Duras's utopian vision presupposes the destruction of all fixed individual and group identities which she described as 'la promotion de la personne séparée de son personnage'[10] (Duras 1996: 67–8).

Despite her commitment to the values of the May movement, Duras strongly criticised the treatment of women in the aftermath of May '68, as she believed that they had once again been silenced by male theoretical voices, speaking on their behalf and excluding any understanding of gender oppression from their retrospective analysis of this period in contemporary French history. For Duras, on the other hand, it was time to abandon the old theoretical models to allow new ways of being and relating to arise. It is true, however, that even within the mixed political groupings of the May movement itself, women were commonly excluded from discussions by their male comrades and relegated to the 'feminine' tasks of making coffee and washing the dishes (Duchen 1986: 7–8). The far-left political currents within the movement, whether Marxist or Maoist, were largely blind to the oppression of women. In response to this, many women felt

10 'the furtherance of the person separate from her or his persona'

that their interests would only be served by the creation of an autonomous, women-only liberation movement. By the early 1970s, the Mouvement de libération des femmes (MLF) had appeared on the French political and cultural scene as a movement which combined activism and practical projects, such as women's refuges, with theoretical concerns about the origins of oppression and strategies for women's liberation. Throughout the 1970s, Marguerite Duras supported the MLF by lending her voice to its cause, but, unlike Simone de Beauvoir, she never became an active participant within the movement. Her reluctance in this respect can perhaps be explained as stemming from her aversion to all political ideologies which she had acquired during her years as a Communist. This does not mean, however, that Duras was not a feminist. On the contrary, in the 1970s, she was a regular contributor to the feminist magazine *Sorcières* and in 1974 she published *Les Parleuses*, a series of talks with Xavière Gauthier about her novels and films, set in a feminist framework. Duras's feminism thus exerted its influence through her ideas, expressed in her work, rather than through active political militancy.

However, this ambivalent attitude to both Communist and feminist politics was by no means the only contradiction discernible in the life and work of Duras. Having spent her childhood and adolescence in Vietnam, she often expressed a feeling of alienation from any concept of French national identity and a sense of not quite belonging to France. As she said in a television interview with Luce Perrot: 'Je pensais partir de France, souvent, quitter ça. Peut-être que je ne me suis jamais tout à fait habituée à ce pays'[11] (Perrot 1988). Her dual identity and cultural background certainly also shaped her work in the cinema, to the extent that her films are 'French' in so far as they are francophone and were made in France. They are not, however, tied to any specific notions of national identity, but cross over national boundaries in a movement towards universality. Similar ambiguities surface when we attempt to situate the films of Duras in the context of French national cinema and the various categories and definitions that have been devised to chart its recent history.

---

11 'I often thought about going away from France, leaving all this. Perhaps I never really got used to this country.'

Duras in contemporary French cinema

Duras's first venture into the world of cinema came in 1959 when Alain Resnais, following his success with *Nuit et brouillard* (1955), asked her to write the script for a film about Hiroshima. Although other well-known novelists, such as Simone de Beauvoir, had been suggested as scriptwriters for Resnais's project, he was certain that Duras's style would be more appropriate to his vision of the film. In the previous year, with her novel *Moderato cantabile*, Duras had developed her literary technique in a direction which departed radically from the traditional models of the novel. The sparsity of descriptive detail and the shift from narration to dialogue facilitated her gradual move to the cinema. The script for *Hiroshima mon amour* (1959) resembles *Moderato cantabile* in so far as both texts hinge on a dual narrative structure. *Hiroshima* tells of the brief love affair between a Japanese man and a French actress, played by Emmanuelle Riva, and which takes place at Hiroshima more than ten years after the genocide caused by the atomic bomb. During their encounters at Hiroshima, the French woman remembers her experience during the Second World War when, at Nevers in France, she was in love with a German soldier. She tells the Japanese man about her torment when her lover died in her arms and she was then publicly humiliated and punished for her perceived betrayal of France. The film projects a complex system of mirrors, in which two places and two love stories as well as the collective memory of Hiroshima and the French woman's individual experience reflect one another. This reflexivity is foregrounded through the constant oscillating movement in the film, as images of the victims of the atom bomb are interspersed with scenes evoking the French woman's relationship with both the Japanese and the German man. In this way, the film itself incorporates elements typical of the work of Duras, such as the coexistence of past and present, memory and oblivion, love and death. Although primarily known as the scriptwriter for *Hiroshima*, Duras was also actively involved in making the film in which Resnais experimented with innovative techniques, such as the use of the off-screen voice. *Hiroshima* was first shown at the Cannes Film Festival in 1959, alongside *Orfeu Negro* by Marcel Camus and François Truffaut's *Les 400 coups* and later became an enormously successful film. It was praised unanimously in *Cahiers du cinéma*, and Godard even confessed that 'je me souviens d'avoir été très jaloux d'*Hiroshima mon amour*[12] (Frodon 1995: 27).

Considering that the 1959 festival coincided with the inception of the *nouvelle vague*, Duras's cinematographic career may be linked, at least historically, with this important phase in the history of French cinema. It is true that Duras's filmic style in the 1970s retained certain aspects reminiscent of the New Wave. From 1973 onwards, her use of desynchronisation, for instance, is consistent with the practices of the New Wave filmmakers in their opposition to the realism of dominant mainstream cinema and its false claim that films are, or should be, a representation of real life. To counteract this claim, directors associated with the New Wave, typically appeared in their own films, in order to highlight the status of cinema as an art form and not as a transparent reflection of the world. Duras also adopted this technique, for example when she appeared in *Le Camion* (1977) or when she chose her own house at Neauphle-le-Château near Paris as the setting for *Nathalie Granger* (1972). Despite these similarities between Duras and the New Wave, there are also a number of important differences which make it difficult to slot her work into this category. First of all, Durassian cinema does not deal explicitly with contemporary social and political issues, least of all consumerism and technology, which Susan Hayward identifies as one of the defining features of the New Wave and, in a wider context, of the postmodern cinema that spans the period from 1958 to the 1990s (Hayward 1993: 206–8). Although many of Duras's films are shaped by underlying political concerns, the latter are never represented directly, but are instead woven into a highly idiosyncratic mixture of autobiography, politics and aesthetics. Nor did Duras wish to be part of what Hayward has called the *entre-hommes* (Hayward 1993: 232), the fraternity of male directors who, in their own work, typically quoted from and referred to the films of others within their own circle. Duras's cinema, on the other hand, is largely self-referential, as her films reflect not only each other, but also the array of images and figures that inhabit her novels and plays. Since her entry into the cinema was precipitated by her collaboration with Resnais, it might be suggested that, like Resnais, Varda and Colpi, Duras is closer to *le nouveau cinéma* (new cinema), than to the New Wave. Truffaut suggested two major characteristics by which to distinguish the two groupings. First, while the

12 'I remember feeling very jealous of *Hiroshima mon amour*.'

New Wave focuses on filming action, new cinema is more concerned with filming ideas and has a stronger and more self-conscious relationship with other art forms. Second, new cinema in the 1950s was influenced by contemporary developments in French literature, in particular the new novel. As the writers associated with the new novel, such as Robbe-Grillet, Simon and, briefly, Duras herself, had their work published by *Minuit*, Truffaut referred to the new cinema as the 'cinéma des éditions de Minuit' (Frodon 1995: 28). However, even though in the mid to late 1950s critics were keen to include Duras in the group of new novel writers, she herself resisted such categorisation of her work. Furthermore, while the new novel and the new cinema may well be defined in terms of a shared concern with ideas, neither Duras's writing nor her cinema constitute a predominantly intellectual enterprise. Indeed, Duras herself explicitly denounced so-called 'intellectual' cinema, in particular that which met with the approval of the *Cahiers* group of critics (Duras 1993: 177). Rather than the intellect, her work invokes desire and passion, precisely the forces which, in Western patriarchal cultures, have been associated with darkness, chaos and the 'feminine' world of the emotions, as opposed to the ordered structures of 'masculine' reason. Thus, although Duras may be loosely associated with the new cinema, such a classification would be too limiting to do justice to her work. Similarly, despite certain elements shared with the New Wave, Duras goes beyond the confines of this movement. Hence a broader definition to describe her work in the context of contemporary French cinema is required, and I would agree here with Susan Hayward that Duras can be considered part of the 1970s avant-garde with which she shares a commitment to 'subvert the political and aesthetic hegemonies' (Hayward 1993: 206).

One of the principle objectives of Duras's cinema was precisely to dismantle power structures, manifest both in society and in certain art forms, including mainstream cinema, which serves largely to reflect and reproduce dominant belief systems. This is nowhere more apparent than in the relationship between her films and French feminism in the 1970s. Her consistent opposition to patriarchal filmmaking practices means that she can definitely be considered part of the wave of 'counter-cinema', created by women directors in France, across other European countries and in the United States. Made just prior to the new wave of feminism, Duras's *Détruire dit-elle* can be seen as an implicit example of such counter-cinema, since the film includes, among other elements, a critique of the patriarchal confinement of women. The first explicit expression of Durassian counter-cinema was *Nathalie Granger* in which Duras consciously devised new ways of filming women in a predominantly female environment. This emphasis on a self-contained women-only world is reminiscent of the separatist current in 1970s feminism and, in retrospect, led Duras to criticise her own work by suggesting that perhaps *Nathalie Granger* was too didactic, almost like a lesson to other, presumably male filmmakers, on how to film women other than through the lens of patriarchal femininity: 'C'est un petit peu le cinéma des autres revu et corrigé, *Nathalie Granger*'[13] (Duras and Gauthier 1974: 73). Although her subsequent films no longer present an obviously feminist agenda at the diegetic level, her cinematic style is consistent with a feminist aesthetic that questions patriarchal cinema and, in particular, its representations of the female body and sexuality.

Despite her insistence that her cinema has not been influenced by any other contemporary *cinéastes* and that her own writing is the only reference that informs her films (Bonnet and Fieschi 1977: 25), there are nevertheless a number of directors with whose work Duras felt a strong affinity. It is evident, for example, that she shared a great deal of mutual admiration with Jean-Luc Godard whom she described as 'le plus grand catalyseur du cinéma mondial'[14] (Duras 1996: 54) and who, for his part, supported and praised her work, in particular *Le Camion* (Godard 1980: 17). Certain aspects of Godard's technique can also be aligned with Durassian cinema. For instance, in a text on his cinema he commented that film, instead of projecting a rapid sequence of images, should foreground each shot as a separate moment, thereby encouraging the spectator to create his own images (Godard 1980: 10). This is certainly congruent with the importance in Duras's cinema of the spectator's role as active creator rather than as passive consumer. Moreover, Godard's decomposition of shots into isolated gestures and movements through the use of slow motion is reminiscent of the extremely slow rhythm and the regular use of fixed frames typical of many films by Duras. Apart from Godard, Duras also greatly admired Bresson, especially his film *Pickpocket* (1959) which, in an

---

13 '*Nathalie Granger* is a bit like looking at and correcting other people's cinema.'
14 'the greatest catalyst in world cinema'

article originally published in *Cinéma* in 1964, she described as 'l'événement cinématographique pour moi le plus considérable de ces dix années'[15] (Duras 1993: 176). There are clear parallels between the work of Bresson and that of Duras, in the sense that for both cinema is essentially a form of poetry rather than the realist representation of believable plots and characters. Duras shares with Bresson what René Prédal has called 'une élégance minimaliste'[16] (Prédal 1991: 58) and, recalling Godard, the view that the filmic image should not function as a logical link within a diegetic chain, but rather as a poetic sign that can generate a whole spectrum of meanings. Thus, although Duras cannot be easily accommodated within any of the available categories that define contemporary French cinema, it may be concluded that her strongest affinities are with avant-garde and experimental cinema as well as with the production of a feminist-inspired counter-cinema. Having outlined the broader context of her work as a director, I will now trace the evolution of her career in film throughout the 1970s.

From literature to film

After her collaboration with Resnais in 1959, subsequent excursions into the world of cinema came in 1961 when Duras wrote the script for Henri Colpi's film *Une aussi longue absence* and in 1966 when she co-directed *La Musica* with Paul Seban. At that time Duras was still primarily a writer and was publishing a series of highly successful novels, among them *Le Ravissement de Lol V Stein* and *Le Vice-consul* which provided the narrative material for *India Song* and *Son nom de Venise dans Calcutta désert*. As Borgomano has pointed out, from the mid-1950s onwards, Duras's writing blurs the generic boundaries between novels and plays, as her involvement with the theatre gradually brings her closer to the cinema. Eventually the narrative of the conventional novel disappears altogether and is replaced by the female voice, first in her plays and then in her films (Borgomano 1985: 29). I would add that the vital importance of sound generally in the work of Duras may well have contributed to her change in direction from writer to director. The emotional and physical resonance of

15 'the most considerable cinematographic event for me in the last ten years'
16 'a minimalist elegance'

music or of the human cry, central to novels like *Moderato cantabile*, *Le Ravissement* and *Le Vice-consul*, cannot be conveyed directly through the abstract form of the written word and, therefore, needs the cinema to bring it to life. If Duras's fiction had already predisposed her towards the cinema, what ultimately motivated her to become a director was her disappointment with the filmic adaptations of her novels by others. In 1958 René Clément produced a film based on *Un barrage*, followed in 1960 by Peter Brook's famous adaptation of *Moderato cantabile* which starred Jean-Paul Belmondo and Jeanne Moreau. In 1967 two further films drawing on Duras's work were released, *Dix heures et demie du soir en été* by Jules Dassin and *Le Marin de Gibraltar* by Tony Richardson. In Duras's own view, none of these films did justice to her texts, since they all followed realist models of representation, distorting the very essence of her art which is not to represent the external world, but to suggest her characters' often unexpressed feelings about and reactions to that world. A second important factor that led Duras to abandon literature and turn to the cinema was her perception of what she called 'the danger of writing'. For Duras, writing was like entering into a space of total darkness and isolation, where she was sometimes gripped by her fear of insanity. Making a film, on the other hand, involves working with a large team and was, therefore, a much less risky enterprise than writing. As she explained to Nicole Bernheim: 'Quand tu fais un film, c'est beaucoup moins dangereux. Tu es quelquefois angoissée, tu as une équipe qu'il faut faire tourner, tu as des problèmes techniques énormes, etc ... mais tu n'es jamais seule face à ce danger'[17] (Bernheim 1974: 39).

Following the release of her first two films, *La Musica* which she co-directed with Paul Seban in 1966 and *Détruire, dit-elle* in 1969, Duras made seventeen films, including her most acclaimed productions *Nathalie Granger* (1972), *Le Camion* (1977) and, of course, *India Song* (1975). Like other directors, Duras faced the economic difficulties that beset experimental cinema in France in the 1970s and 1980s, as all her films were made on relatively low budgets. To finance the production of *Nathalie Granger*, for instance, she received only ten million old francs from the Centre national de la cinématographie (CNC), at a time when the average sum given to directors was forty to

17 'When you make a film, it's much less dangerous. You sometimes feel stressed, you've got a team to run, you've got enormous technical problems, etc... but you're never on your own with this danger.'

fifty million francs. The financial problems that Duras experienced throughout her career in cinema are compounded by the fact that some of her early films, like *Détruire dit-elle* and *La Femme du Gange* (1973) have become virtually inaccessible to the viewing public, while *Jaune le Soleil*, made in 1971, was never distributed.[18] Two Duras retrospectives, in 1992 and in 1998, have rekindled both public and critical interest which may encourage the institutions of French cinema to make her work more widely available. And yet, despite financial constraints and her marginal position in French cinema, Duras remained determined to develop her own filmic style and to reject any involvement in commercial cinema which treats the viewer as a passive consumer. As she said in an interview with Michelle Porte: 'But this cinema, once it is ended, leaves nothing, nothing after it. It is erased the moment it's through. While mine, it seems to me, begins the next day, like something read' (Porte 1983: 60). In its aversion to direct representation and narration, her work is diametrically opposed to what she called 'le cinéma quantitatif' which tirelessly reproduces the same basic plots and whose success is measured in terms of the number of spectators it attracts. Duras, on the other hand, saw herself as belonging to the 'cinéma d'auteur' (Duras 1996: 36–8). This does not suggest, however, that she aligned herself with the bourgeois notion of the 'auteur' as a solitary individual creator. On the contrary, she always stressed the vital importance of the team of artists who worked on her films, and she participated in collaborative texts which underscore the contributions made by each member of her team. Thus *India Song* was followed by Nicole Bernheim's book *Marguerite Duras tourne un film* which comprises a series of interviews, not only with Duras but also with the actors, the make-up artist, the chief electrician and others who were involved in making the film. The notion of auteurism also becomes problematic in view of the fact that, in the French context at least, the auteur is usually male and that women directors have no coherent tradition of female authorship in cinema. In relation to Duras, therefore, it would be appropriate to follow Judith Mayne who, citing Claire Johnston, provides a broad definition of auteurism as the 'narrative and visual system associated with a given director' (Mayne 1990: 96). To describe Durassian

18 For this reason, my discussions of Duras's cinema in this book focus on nine films which represent key works in her cinematographic production and which remain available on video, either in the United Kingdom or in France.

auteurism, however, this classification needs to be expanded to include the primary function of sound, and in particular of the voice, which will be discussed in the next chapter.

Towards the end of the 1970s, after a decade of experimentation with image, sound and text in the cinema, Duras decided to abandon gradually her work as a director and to return to writing. While cinema had enabled her to explore a visual and sonorous space beyond the written word, she felt increasingly constrained by film, particularly by what she perceived as its intrusive visibility. In 1979, in the preface to the script of *Le Navire Night*, she described her disillusionment with cinema in the following terms: 'Cinéma, fini. J'allais recommencer à écrire des livres, j'allais revenir au pays natal, à ce labeur terrifiant que j'avais quitté depuis dix ans [...] Je me reposais d'une victoire, celle d'avoir enfin atteint l'impossibilité de filmer'[19] (Duras 1979: 14–15). If *Détruire dit-elle* had launched Duras on the French film scene in 1969, her exit was precipitated by the virtual destruction of representation itself in *L'Homme atlantique* (1981) in which, for half of the film's duration, we see a black screen while listening to a reading of the text *L'Homme atlantique*. Following this event, which Michelle Royer aptly described as 'une véritable mise à mort du cinéma'[20] (Royer 1997: 18), Duras's career as a director came to an end in 1985 when, jointly with Jean-Marc Turine and her son Jean Mascolo, she made her last film *Les Enfants*.

References

Adler, L. (1998), *Marguerite Duras*, Paris, Gallimard.
Bernheim, N. (1974), 'Autour d'un film – *India Song*', *Revue du cinéma*, 291: 38–60.
Bernheim, N. (1981), *Marguerite Duras tourne un film*, Paris, Albatros.
Bonnet, J. and Fieschi, J. (1977), 'Marguerite Duras', *Cinématographe*, 32: 25–8.
Borgomano, M. (1985), *L'Ecriture filmique de Marguerite Duras*, Paris, Albatros.
Coward, D. (1999), 'Light from a dying star', *Times Literary Supplement*, 21 May, 6–7.

19 'The cinema was finished. I was going to start writing books again. I was going to return to my native land, to that terrifying labour that I had left behind ten years ago [...] I was resting after a victory, the victory of having finally achieved the impossibility of making films.'
20 'a veritable murder of the cinema'

Duchen, C. (1986), *Feminism in France from May '68 to Mitterrand*, London, Routledge & Kegan Paul.

Duras, M. (1950), *Un barrage contre le Pacifique*, Paris, Gallimard.

Duras, M. (1969), *Détruire dit-elle*, Paris, Minuit.

Duras, M. (1977), *Le Camion*, Paris, Minuit.

Duras, M. (1979), *Le Navire Night – Césarée – Les Main négatives – Aurélia Steiner – Aurélia Steiner – Aurélia Steiner*, Paris, Mercure de France.

Duras, M. (1984), *L'Amant*, Paris, Minuit.

Duras, M. (1985), *La Douleur*, Paris, POL.

Duras, M. (1993), *Le Monde extérieur*, Paris, POL.

Duras, M. (1996), *Les Yeux verts*, Paris, Coll. Cahiers du cinéma, Editions de l'Etoile.

Duras, M. and Gauthier, X. (1974), *Les Parleuses*, Paris, Minuit.

Duras, M. and Mitterrand, F. (1986), 'Le bureau de poste de la rue Dupin', *L'Autre Journal*, 5 March 1986, 32–40.

Duras, M. and Porte, M. (1977), *Les Lieux de Marguerite Duras*, Paris, Minuit.

Frodon, J. M. (1995), *L'Age moderne du cinéma français*, Paris, Flammarion.

Godard, J.-L. (1980), 'Propos rompus', *Cahiers du cinéma*, 316: 10–17.

Hayward, S. (1993), *French National Cinema*, London, Routledge.

Holmes, D. and Ingram, R., *French Film Directors: François Truffaut*, Manchester, Manchester University Press.

Lamy, S. and Roy, A. (1981), *Marguerite Duras à Montréal*, Montréal, Editions Spirale.

Lebelley, F. (1994), *Duras ou le poids d'une plume*, Paris, Grasset.

Mayne, J. (1990), *The Woman at the Keyhole: Feminism and Women's Cinema*, Bloomington, Indiana University Press.

Perrot, L. (1988), *Au-delà des pages*, no. 4, TF1.

Porte, M. (1983), 'The Places of Marguerite Duras', *Enclitic*, 7(2): 55–62.

Prédal, R. (1991), *Le Cinéma français depuis 1945*, Paris, Editions Nathan.

Royer, M. (1997), *L'Ecran de la passion: une étude du cinéma de Marguerite Duras*, Mount Nebo, Queensland, Boombana Publications.

2

Words and images: filming desire

Although for Duras writing and filmmaking were closely linked, her work cannot be considered as that of a writer who adapted her books to the screen by simply translating fictional plots, characters and settings into film narratives. As we have seen, she criticised other directors for adopting this procedure in their attempts to transform her novels into mainstream cinema. Instead, her aim was to transcend the limitations of both literature and cinema by creating what Borgomano has called an *écriture filmique* (Borgomano 1985: 9), a cinematographic form of writing which would explore the interface between text and film and which, at its most fundamental level, is reflected in the relationship between words and images. In Duras's written texts words are important in their own right, rather than as subordinate elements in syntactic and narrative sequences. Speaking to Xavière Gauthier about language in relation to her own creative process, Duras commented: 'Le mot compte plus que la syntaxe. C'est avant tout des mots, sans articles d'ailleurs, qui viennent et qui s'imposent. Le temps grammatical suit, d'assez loin'[1] (Duras and Gauthier 1974: 11). Individual words, therefore, instead of simply contributing to the overall meaning of a sentence, generate their own meanings by weaving complex webs of associations in relation to other words. Moreover, for Duras the function of the word as a poetic sign is not so much to represent the outside world as to engage the reader in her characters' inner experience. This move away from literature as a

[1] 'The word counts for more than the syntax. It's words without articles that come and impose themselves first of all. The grammatical tenses follow quite a bit later.'

representation of external reality corresponds to her anti-realist, anti-narrative cinema which transposes the poetic quality of her texts on to the filmic image. One of the striking features of Duras's shots, particularly in *India Song*, is their length and the predominance of fixed frames over tracking shots. Because of their sparsity and static quality, these images are reminiscent of photographs or paintings, unlike the clutter of moving pictures in mainstream cinema which Duras described as 'suffocating' (Duras and Gauthier 1974: 87). Like her words, Duras's images do not operate as so many links within the film narrative, but rather as signs which produce their own meanings in relation to other images and to the soundtrack. They often function as metaphors to reveal a hidden, inner world which Duras called 'l'ombre interne' (the inner shadow). Since this is a shared human world, the images that suggest it are typically devoid of concrete details in relation to characters, setting and narrative. The image in a Duras film, then, privileges the general over the particular, the universal over the individual and thus presents a certain archetypal quality, by comparison with the narrowly realist imagery of mainstream cinema.

In both her writing and filmmaking practices, Duras attached great importance to the imaginative process of her readers and spectators. Unlike a written text which can generate an infinite number of representations in the reader's mind, the filmic image tends to restrict the imagination, precisely because whatever is visually present in front of the spectator, on the cinema screen, cannot be imagined. 'Le cinéma arrête le texte, frappe de mort sa descendance: l'imaginaire',[2] as Duras said in *Le Camion* (Duras 1977: 75). Thus, paradoxically, for the imagination to become fully engaged, the image needs to be absent, as in *L'Homme atlantique*, or at least relatively empty. From *India Song* onwards one of Duras's main concerns was to create images which, through their lack of descriptive detail and precise representation, would liberate the spectator's imagination. In the same way as the openness of her texts allows the reader to invent her or his own versions of these works, the spacious quality of the shots invites viewers to participate actively in recreating her films by projecting their own mental images on to the screen.

2 'The cinema stops the text and kills its offspring: the imagination.'

Desynchronisation: the divided self

The most innovative and enduring of Duras's techniques in the cinema is desynchronisation and, in particular, her use of the *voix off*.[3] She first experimented with this device in the 1973 film *La Femme du Gange* and employed it consistently in all the films that will be investigated in the remainder of this chapter, from *India Song* to *Aurélia Steiner (Vancouver)*. In the text of *La Femme du Gange* Duras refers to the split between the soundtrack and the image-track as constituting two separate films, 'the film of the voice' and 'the film of the image' (Duras 1973: 103). But this discontinuity is not just purely formal, since it affects the production of meaning within the films themselves. For the voices do not correspond in a literal sense to the images on screen, in so far as they do not provide a commentary on or an explanation of the latter. In *Son nom de Venise dans Calcutta désert*, for instance, the meanings that may emerge from the relationship between voices and images are largely metaphorical and need to be interpreted as such by the spectator who is required to contribute actively towards creating an understanding of the film. In mainstream cinema, moreover, the use of synchronisation facilitates the spectator's identification with the actors on screen who appear to represent 'real' individuals. As Michelle Royer has pointed out, in Duras's films, on the other hand, the dissociation between the actors' physical presence on and their voices off-screen destroys the 'reality effect' of synchronisation (Royer 1997: 34). Duras's filmic technique, then, illustrates her view that cinema is not a transparent reflection of the world, but a highly complex construct which should be presented as such. But the gap between voice and image does more than merely show the artificial nature of cinema. It also creates an unsettling feeling of dislocation within the spectator's own sense of identity which, for the duration of the film, loses its usual cohesion and unity. Duras's films demonstrate that the notion of a stable coherent self or 'subject' is, in fact, an illusion which, in Western patriarchal cultures at least, has been used by dominant social groups to reinforce their position of power over those who have been defined as ' the object', 'the other'. In the context of mainstream cinema, for example, the subject might be the male spectator who is invited to control the female object on screen with his

3 The *voix off* in Durassian cinema refers to one or several voices which are heard off-screen and which often read the text that accompanies the film's visual track.

gaze. The mechanism of desynchronisation, on the other hand, shatters this construct of the unified subject, as the spectator's position in relation to the film is split between seeing and hearing, images and voices, presence and absence, on and off-screen. Seen from this perspective, the use of the *voix off* could be said to carry an implicitly political significance, in the sense that it questions the oppositional categories that underpin the hierarchical structures of society.

Perhaps the most fundamental impulse which underscores Duras's writing and her films is precisely this desire to overcome divisions and oppositions, both in society at large and in individual relationships. The experience of separation and distance between people is a central theme in her work, counterbalanced by an equally powerful need to transcend such barriers. Moving beyond the self and towards the other represents the essence of Duras's understanding of desire which, in its extreme form, may lead to the loss of self either through madness or death. This notion of desire as the fusion of self and other is often translated into a passionate love affair, such as the legendary *coup de foudre* which strikes Anne-Marie Stretter and Michael Richardson in *Le Ravissement de Lol V. Stein*. More generally, however, desire in Duras signifies her protagonists' wish to join and merge with the generality of human experience, which Dominique Noguez has described as a profoundly spiritual dimension of her work (Noguez 1978: 37). This dialectical movement between difference and separation, on the one hand, and the desire to attain a fusional symbiotic state of being, on the other, is reflected in Duras's cinematographic technique itself. While the use of desynchronisation initially provokes a disturbing feeling of dissociation in the spectator, the gap between voice and image transports us to a different space which is located beyond our usual, predominantly visual experience. Michel Chion in *La Voix au cinéma* has argued that the gaze always implies the perception of distance between the viewer as subject of the gaze and the visual representations on the screen as its object. Hearing, on the other hand, because it reduces or even abolishes this distance, creates a sense of proximity between viewer and viewed. This observation certainly applies to Duras's cinema where the subject/object division becomes blurred, so that our attention is focused simultaneously on the external presence of the image and on another inner dimension which is activated by the off-screen voice. As Stéphane

Bouquet has observed, this space between 'inside' and 'outside' puts the spectator in a receptive, almost trance-like state in relation to the film (Bouquet 1996: 37).

Throughout her career as a writer, the power of the voice and of speech was a central preoccupation for Duras. In her texts the musical quality of recurring words and the rhythm of the syntax create a powerful resonance so that, as we are reading her work, it is as if we are listening to our own inner voice. Michelle Royer has made a similar point about Duras's writing process which was accompanied by 'une voix qui viendrait de l'intérieur'[4] (Royer 1997: 103). An equally strong emphasis on the voice informed her work in the theatre where she privileged speech over visual representation by having the actors recite their text rather than physically enact their role. Similarly, in her films she sought to foreground the spoken word by separating it from the image through the technique of the *voix off*. This evidently contrasts with the dominant practices in mainstream cinema where the voice is subsumed by the image and where it functions primarily to contribute to the film narrative. In Duras's cinema, on the contrary, the voice is vitally important, for if the visual space on the screen reflects the spectator's conscious mind, then the voice provides access to what she has called 'cet autre espace' (Duras and Gauthier 1974: 191). This 'other space' represents the unconscious, archaic layers of experience which, in psychoanalyic theory, are linked to the early stages of human experience, in particular the mother/child relationship. Given this connection between the voice and the maternal, it is not surprising that Duras's films should privilege the female voice. As Michel Chion has shown, the importance of the spectator's auditory experience in cinema may be due to the fact that the first contact between the infant and its external world is established through the mother's voice (Chion 1993: 29). Of all the senses, then, hearing is the most archaic, since it relates to the stage where the infant does not yet experience her or himself as a separate individual, different from the mother. In relation to Duras's cinema, therefore, the prominence of the female voice translates a desire to return to the maternal and the longing for an imagined state of fusion with the mother. The flowing quality of the voice provides a sense of continuity which contrasts with the fragmentation of the image-track and the sense of separation that

4 'a voice that seemed to come from within'

underpins the use of desynchronisation. While Duras rarely used visual close-ups, the omnipresence of the voice creates a kind of auditory close-up, reactivating in the spectator the experience of proximity and identification suppressed by the relative distance of the images. The intimacy with the voice is particularly striking in those films where Duras's own voice appears on the sound-track. This idiosyncrasy might be interpreted as a form of narcissism, with Duras posturing as the all-powerful mother in relation to her spectators. However, such a view would ignore the fact that, although the voice itself is immediately recognisable as that of Duras, in her films she never speaks from the assumed position of the all-knowing director, the 'auteur' as an authority figure. Rather, through her reading of the texts she lends her voice to the protagonists' stories or even to the protagonists themselves, as in the case of *Aurélia Steiner*. The vocal presence in these films, then, is both familiar and strange, in so far as we are listening to a voice which is and is not that of Duras.

India Song

Duras's most popular and highly acclaimed film was first shown at the 1975 Cannes Film Festival, where it received the Prix de l'association française des cinémas d'art et d'essai (a prize for art and experimental cinema). Surprisingly, given its title, *India Song* was shot in four different locations, all in or near Paris: the Trianon palace at Versailles, the tennis courts at the village of Neauphle-le-Château, two flats in Paris and the Rothschild's former palace in the Bois de Boulogne. The fact that Duras filmed India in the middle of Paris may be explained in two ways. First, there were the usual financial constraints, for although she was given more money for *India Song* than for her other films, the sum she received was still only equivalent to that usually allocated to short films. Second, the idea of shooting the film 'on location' would have gone against the grain of her primary objective as a director. For the aim of the film was to evoke in the spectator's mind an impression of the places mentioned, for example Calcutta, Lahore, Laos, and not to show realistic images of the actual locations themselves. For similar reasons, the geographical references in the film are frequently inaccurate, since what Duras wanted to create was an imaginary, not a real geography (Duras and Gauthier 1974: 169).

India Song has its origins in three literary texts, *Le Ravissement de Lol V. Stein* (1964), *Le Vice-consul* (1965) and *L'Amour* (1971). In a cinematic context it is related to the 1973 film *La Femme du Gange* and, more importantly, to *Son nom de Venise dans Calcutta désert* (1976). *India Song* is, therefore, part of a cycle of works that revolve around the same stories and protagonists, that is Lol V. Stein, the vice-consul, the beggarwoman from Laos and, of course, Anne-Marie Stretter. In the key scene of *Le Ravissement de Lol V. Stein*, set at a summer ball, Michael Richardson abandons his fiancée, Lola Valérie Stein, when he falls in love with Anne-Marie Stretter whom he later follows to Calcutta. Elements from this novel have been transposed on to *India Song* where, in the early part of the film, the two female voices refer back to the story of Lol. The ball at S. Tahla is displaced on to the central scene in *India Song*, as we see Anne-Marie Stretter (Delphine Seyrig) dancing at the reception given by her husband at the French embassy in Calcutta. At various points in the film, the off-screen voices provide the spectator with clues concerning Anne-Marie Stretter's past. We gather, for instance, that she originally came from Venice, that she was a musician and that her maiden name, which she took from her mother, was Anna-Maria Guardi. As a young woman, she was exiled from Europe to Asia when she married a colonial administrator from Savannakhet in Laos. She later met Mr Stretter, the French ambassador to India, and, for seventeen years, followed him round the capitals of Asia. She finally committed suicide by drowning herself in the sea near Calcutta. This skeletal and fragmented outline of Anne-Marie Stretter's trajectory demonstrates that Duras was not interested in constructing a coherent film narrative. Instead, as we will see, these details regarding the heroine's external circumstances were intended primarily as signs of her underlying emotional experience and of the implicit connections that link her to the other main figures in the film.

India Song can be divided into three parts. During the first section, the two female voices speak about the beggarwoman and the vice-consul from Lahore and recall the events at the ball surrounding Lol V. Stein, Anne-Marie Stretter and Michael Richardson. The second part of the film evokes the reception at the French embassy, accompanied by a multitude of off-screen voices commenting on Anne-Marie Stretter and the vice-consul. The final section is set in a mythical place referred to as 'the islands' where Anne-Marie Stretter is seen first in the Prince of Wales hotel, accompanied by her four suitors, and then at the French residence, just prior to her death. Her suicide, however, is not represented but merely implied, as Duras's off-screen voice comments: 'C'est sur la plage qu'on a retrouvé son peignoir'.[5]

If *India Song* ends with this reference to suicide, several clues in the opening scenes lead the spectator to assume that Anne-Marie Stretter is already dead when the film begins and that the latter is, therefore, an imaginary reconstruction of the last few weeks or months of her life. Indeed, the voices confirm that she was found dead, one night, and that she is now buried in the English cemetery. The visual track alludes to this with a long shot of a photograph, a candle and flowers placed on top of a piano which, given the vital importance of music for Anne-Marie Stretter, might be seen as a symbolic shrine to Duras's heroine. Duras herself spoke of this image as representing 'what I call the altar, it's dedicated to her memory, to Anne-Marie Stretter' (Duras and Porte 1983: 56). The thematic emphasis in *India Song* on separation, absence and death is mirrored in the film's particular use of desynchronisation. For not only did Duras redeploy the disembodied off-screen voices familiar from the previous film *La Femme du Gange*, but she also filmed the actors' physical presence dissociated from their voices. While directing the film, she recorded the actors' reading the entire text of *India Song* which was then played back during the filming of each scene. Thus, throughout the film, the actors do not speak but instead listen to their own recorded voices, as they perform the prescribed movements and gestures (Duras 1980: 43). In this way, *India Song* generates a radical fracture between the voice-off and the body on-screen, making the actors appear like spectres or shadows rather than realistic incarnations of the protagonists. This is particularly striking in the case of Anne-Marie Stretter whose ghostlike appearance and movements haunt the film. In strictly narrative terms this is, of course, due to the fact that the entire film itself is like a memory, a resurrection of Anne-Marie Stretter. However, in a more general sense, *India Song* exemplifies Duras's views about the role of the actor. Both in her theatre and her cinema the actor's task was not to embody a particular character, but rather to interpret the latter's inner world. This is reminiscent of the plays of Bertolt Brecht where acting was primarily a staged performance,

5 'Her dressing gown was found on the beach.'

recognisable as such to the audience, and not an attempt to tie actors to the assumed identity of the characters they represent. Thus, in *India Song*, although Delphine Seyrig symbolises Anne-Marie Stretter's experience, she does not embody her as a specific individual. The film, then, creates a certain distance between the actress and her character into which the spectator can project her or his own version of 'Anne-Marie Stretter'. This was, in fact, what Seyrig herself did during the making of the film, when she mentally substituted places and people from her own life for those in *India Song*. As she said to Duras in *La Couleur des mots*: 'Anne-Marie Stretter [...] c'était pas ton Anne-Marie Stretter, c'était la mienne'[6] (Duras and Noguez 1984a). The discrepancy between the actor and the protagonist also means that all the actors in the film are, as Duras put it, 'distanced from themselves' (Duras 1980: 43). This disturbing sense of alienation is particularly powerful during the reception scene when we see Anne-Marie Stretter dancing with the young attaché (Mathieu Carrière) while their off-screen voices talk about Venice, music and India: 'Ce n'est ni pénible, ni agréable de vivre aux Indes. Ni facile, ni difficile. Ce n'est rien. Vous voyez, rien'.[7] Neither of the actors speak on-screen, but instead listen to their own voices on the soundtrack, almost as if they were listening to someone else. This fragmentation of identity is further enhanced through the use of the large mirror which doubles the image of the dancing couple as well as that of other figures throughout the film. The split representation of the protagonists creates a similar division within the spectator. As we are drawn into the mirror we can no longer control the figures on screen as unified objects of our gaze and thus our own self-perception loses its usual coherence. The effect of this process is to allow viewers to temporarily suspend their sense of self and thereby to enter more fully into the protagonists' experience of desire, separation and loss. As Duras has put it: 'I see their absence [that of the actors] as parallel to our own when we gaze at them in the film. And thus, mutually lost, we meet each other' (Duras 1980: 44). For Duras, it is precisely the absence of a separate identity which allows us to connect with others. Therefore the destruction of the self-contained individual in her work is always accompanied by a blurring of the boundaries between self and other.

6 'Anne-Marie Stretter [...] was not your Anne-Marie Stretter, she was mine.'
7 'Living in India is neither unpleasant, nor pleasant. Neither easy, nor difficult. It's nothing. You see, nothing.'

In *India Song* this key theme of self-transcendence is expressed through a chain of associations between the beggarwoman, the vice-consul and Anne-Marie Stretter. The film begins with a long static shot of a sunset, overlaid by the initial credit sequence, and accompanied by a woman's voice, singing, laughing and speaking in her native language. Two other female voices then present fragments of the story with which readers of *Le Vice-consul* are already familiar: the beggarwoman from Savannakhet in Laos who was chased from her home by her own mother, when she fell pregnant at the age of 17. Since then she has walked for ten years across East Asia and has now reached her final destination, Calcutta. Her journey has been one of progressive loss, both physically and mentally. Not only has she joined the beggars and lepers in the park behind the French embassy, waiting for scraps of food from the colonial tables, she has also lost her memory, her identity and, in the eyes of Western society, her mind. However, Duras was generally critical of the idea of 'sanity' prevalent in Western cultures, associated with the 'masculine' principle of rationality and logic. For the very existence of these dominant categories depends on the suppression of their 'feminine' opposites, the emotions, intuition, the unconscious, all of which are considered 'irrational' and thus uncontrollably dangerous.[8] It is not surprising, therefore, that Duras introduced the figure of the beggarwoman, both female and non-European, to question this construct of Western masculinity.[9] In the film, the woman's song, the words of which are incomprehensible to Western audiences, her screams and her laughter represent the 'feminine' mode of expression that exceeds the rational structures of language. Although in a physical sense the beggarwoman is forever separated from her mother and hence her origins, her lack of a coherent rational self suggests that she has returned to a primordial state of existence which Duras described as 'un état animal'[10] (Bernheim 1974: 42). The beggarwoman functions as an allegorical figure, symbolising the universal experience of absence and loss, rather than representing a specific woman. It is for this reason that, although we continuously hear her on the soundtrack, she is

8 For a comprehensive study of madness in Duras, see Udris, 1993.

9 In *Le Vice-consul* it is suggested that the writer Peter Morgan feels threatened by the beggarwoman and that he, therefore, tries to contain and control her through the story he writes about her.

10 'an animal-like state'

never visually present on screen. As Duras said: 'Elle est sans passé, sans avenir, sans bêtise, sans intelligence [...] sans identité. C'est l'instant'[11] (Bernheim 1974: 42).

From a social and political perspective the beggarwoman and Anne-Marie Stretter appear to belong to two completely separate worlds. If the beggarwoman exemplifies the poverty and suffering of colonised India, Anne-Marie Stretter, on the other hand, personifies the affluence of the white colonising classes. However, for Duras the dichotomous categories of 'rich' and 'poor', 'oppressor' and 'oppressed' are reductive, since they do not take into account shared experiences. Anne-Marie Stretter, although well-off in a purely material sense, has been destroyed by her own society which condemned married women to a lifetime of emptiness and suffocating boredom.[12] Although she keeps up her smile and the polite veneer of middle-class etiquette, as one of the guests at the reception remarks, 'on la dirait prisonnière d'une sorte de souffrance'.[13] The numbing monotony of Anne-Marie Stretter's existence, as she progresses towards death, is conveyed by the predominance of fixed frames, the protagonists' slow heavy movements and the repeated references to the stifling heat and the static quality of life in India. Whilst she is still an object of desire for the men who surround her, the film suggests that her own desire and passion, exemplified by her love of music, have been destroyed. Like the beggarwoman who has lost everything, Anne-Marie Stretter has already endured her own psychic death which is then actualised by her suicide. The phrase Duras used to describe the beggarwoman's experience could be applied equally to the other woman: 'Vivante, elle est morte'[14] (Duras and Gauthier 1974: 214). In this respect the only difference between the two seems to be the fact that, while Anne-Marie Stretter is still semiconscious of her suffering and thus chooses suicide as her only possible liberation, the 'mad' beggarwoman has lost all consciousness and can, therefore, survive in a purely physical sense. These links between the two female characters are suggested

11 'She is without a past, without a future, without stupidity, without intelligence [...] without identity. She is the moment.'
12 There is an interesting parallel here with Duras's autobiographical novel *L'Amant* where she describes the deadly monotony endured by married women in the colonies and which drove many of them to suicide.
13 'she seemed imprisoned by a kind of suffering'
14 'She died while still alive.'

by the film's visual and verbal juxtapositions of their respective stories when, towards the end of the opening shot, the voices suddenly switch from their narration of the beggarwoman's story to that of Anne-Marie Stretter. Here, the narrative transition is made through verbal references to Calcutta, the place where both women arrive at the end of their journey: 'A Calcutta elles étaient ensemble, la blanche et l'autre'.[15] In synchrony with this comment on the soundtrack, the camera pans from the outside to the inside, replacing the sunset with the décor of the French embassy, while a series of metonymic shots focus on objects that suggest the ghostly presence of Anne-Marie Stretter: a red dress, jewellery and a wig.[16] Throughout the film, the beggarwoman is associated primarily with the 'outside', both literally, as her screams and laughter accompany the images of the embassy gardens, and metaphorically, since she represents the excluded 'other' of colonial society. But Anne-Marie Stretter, although she is filmed almost exclusively on inside locations, signalling her status within that society, also occupies the position of the 'outsider', in so far as she transgresses the bourgeois model of the 'respectable wife' because of her relationship with Michael Richardson and, as the film implies, her affairs with the various other men who surround her at the embassy.

The experience of exclusion, common to the two female figures in *India Song*, is equally shared by the male protagonist, the vice-consul of Lahore (Michael Lonsdale). The eponymous hero of Duras's 1965 novel has been marginalised by his social milieu, following an incident at Lahore where he shot at the lepers in the Shalimar gardens and then at his own reflection in the mirror, a violent gesture expressing his rage at the senselessness of human suffering, both that of India and his own. Like the beggarwoman, he is perceived as a threat to the false stability of the colonial bourgeoisie which attempts to contain them both by categorising them as 'mad'. Furthermore, his own social and personal alienation enables him to develop a tacit understanding of Anne-Marie Stretter, the object of his unrequited love: 'Nous n'avons rien à nous dire. Nous sommes les mêmes'.[17]

---

15 'At Calcutta they were together, the white woman and the other one.'

16 The term 'metonymic shot' is used here to describe the visual representation of objects which, through their association with a specific person, come to stand for that person.

17 'We have nothing to say to each other. We are the same.''

Throughout the film, the latent similarities between the three central figures are suggested by an almost imperceptible slippage of both soundtrack and image-track. A striking illustration of this technique of displacement is a long 'take' in the first part of *India Song* where the camera frames Anne-Marie Stretter stretched out on the floor, in a lifeless posture, alongside Michael Richardson (Claude Mann) and another man, described as 'un invité des Stretter' (a guest of the Stretters – Didier Flamand). The focus then shifts to a close-up of the vice-consul in tears, as he looks at Anne-Marie Stretter, while the off-screen voices comment on this man who has never been able to speak to or even approach the woman he desires. The anguish of rejection experienced by the male character is thus visually juxtaposed with the woman's mental and emotional suffering which, at an earlier moment within the same sequence, had been described as 'une lèpre du cœur'.[18] The connection between Anne-Marie Stretter and the vice-consul is further emphasised as the camera oscillates between the woman, sitting on the floor in her dressing gown, and the man outside in the park, touching her red bicycle as a substitute object of desire. Towards the end of this section, the synthesis between these two protagonists is extended to include the beggarwoman whose chant on the soundtrack accompanies images of Anne-Marie Stretter, while the voices recall the vice-consul's killing the lepers of Lahore.

India Song disrupts the realist model in cinema which demands a linear, logical film narrative. Instead, Duras's film is structured like a poem, as the verbal and visual repetitions and associations create a pattern of correspondences between superficially different characters, places and events. Despite their differences in terms of class, race and gender, the beggarwoman, Anne-Marie Stretter and the vice-consul are united by the fact that all three are outsiders, excluded from bourgeois society and exiled from themselves. All three are symbolic figures representing physical and mental suffering, loss and aliena-tion. For Duras, the creation of 'realistic' characters and locations is irrelevant to the purpose of her cinema, since external reality itself is seen as a construct, made up of the different categories and definitions we impose upon the world around us. In *India Song*, by contrast, social, psychological and geographical barriers are broken down, as super-ficial differences dissolve into an understanding of the interrelatedness of all phenomena.

18 'leprosy of the heart'

Son nom de Venise dans Calcutta désert

In the winter of 1975, within a few months of the release of *India Song*, Duras made *Son nom de Venise*, probably the most challenging film at that point in her career. In a filmed interview with Dominique Noguez, Duras questioned her interlocutor's retrospective assessment of *India Song* as her greatest accomplishment in cinema when she claimed that '*Son nom de Venise* c'est ce que j'ai fait de plus important au cinéma'[19] (Duras and Noguez 1984b). Whether or not spectators may share this view, the film is certainly one of Duras's most radical works, as she pursues her destruction of representational cinema. *Son nom de Venise* seems to inscribe the end of desire through the filming of death and disintegration, described by Michelle Royer as 'une esthétique de la décomposition'[20] (Royer 1997: 87). This preoccupation with decay and decomposition is reflected in the location of *Son nom de Venise*, since Duras returned to the crumbling palace in the Bois de Boulogne that had already provided part of the setting of *India Song*. The Rothschild's family home had been abandoned since the Second World War when, in 1942, it was requisitioned and used as the German army's headquarters. Shortly after the filming of *Son nom de Venise* its empty ruins were demolished. Apart from their shared location, *India Song* and *Son nom de Venise* also resemble each other in so far as Duras, in a move unprecedented in cinema, used the same soundtrack for both films, creating an uncanny echo effect which links the two works in the spectator's mind. In *Son nom de Venise*, however, the voices and the music familiar from *India Song* are accompanied by a completely different visual track which destroys the images of the previous film. What is most striking about the second image-track is that it is entirely devoid of human figures, as the movement towards death, begun in *India Song*, is brought to its conclusion. The second film, therefore, is not so much a sequel to as the completion of the first. Whereas in *India Song* the frequent references to death coming from the off-screen voices are counteracted by the protagonists' visual presence on screen, *Son nom de Venise* films their absence, as the camera sweeps through the empty palace, representing the deserted embassy at Calcutta mentioned in the title. As Duras herself remarked: 'L'engloutissement dans la mort et des lieux et des

19 '*Son nom de Venise* is the most important thing I've done in the cinema.'
20 'an aesthetics of decomposition'

gens est *filmé* dans *Son nom de Venise*'[21] (Duras *et al.* 1979: 94). The destruction of people, objects and places is conveyed directly by the shots of cracked paving stones, broken windows, shattered mirrors, mouldy ceilings and broken chimneys which punctuate the film. These shots alternate with images of the park, the trees and the sky, suggesting an opposition between the perennial existence of nature, on the one hand, and the impermanence of human creation and embodiment, on the other hand. Paradoxically, the images of *Son nom de Venise* also serve as a reminder of the ephemeral quality of visual representation, since what survives of the protagonists of *India Song* is merely the memory of their story, preserved and recounted by the voices on the soundtrack. In *Son nom de Venise*, then, text and voice prevail over the image, prefiguring the subsequent development of Durassian cinema.

For some critics there is no relationship at all in *Son nom de Venise* between the images on screen and the words spoken off-screen. René Prédal, for instance, has argued that, at the level of the image, the film is an empty space into which spectators may project their visual memories of *India Song* (Prédal 1991: 279). In other words, *Son nom de Venise* is seen as a pretext for the recreation of *India Song*, in particular of its protagonists, perhaps because the absence of human representation is perceived as a particularly disconcerting feature of the second film. Similarly, Dominique Noguez insists that spectators of the two films will continue to 'see' the scenes and characters from *India Song* in *Son nom de Venise* (Duras and Noguez 1984b). Such an assessment implies that the latter is simply a repetition of the former, not only in terms of the shared soundtrack, but also because it reactivates the viewers' visual memory. A closer study of the film shows, however, that *Son nom de Venise* is not a reproduction of *India Song*, but rather that it generates its own correspondences between the soundtrack and the new image-track and that, therefore, rather than replacing, it displaces *India Song*. That there exists a more than arbitrary correlation in *Son nom de Venise* between sound and image is substantiated by the fact that the shooting of the film was accompanied throughout by the pre-recorded soundtrack (Duras and Noguez 1984b). But, whereas in *India Song* the relationship between words and images is, to some extent, a literal one, in *Son nom de Venise* it is

21 'The swallowing up in death of both places and people is *filmed* in *Son nom de Venise*.'

entirely figurative. Thus, while *India Song* still shows the physical presence of the characters referred to by the voices, the images of *Son nom de Venise* are primarily metaphorical representations, not only of the protagonists' inner world, but also of the broader themes of both films. In the opening credit sequence of the second film, for example, the shots of cracked paving stones juxtaposed with the beggar-woman's song function as a metaphor for the mental fragmentation, the 'madness' which connects her inner world to that of the vice-consul and of Anne-Marie Stretter. When the same paving stones recur later in the film, the image is overlaid this time by the vice-consul's piercing scream of desire and madness. Indeed, the repeated shots of smashed windows, broken glass and cracked mirrors might be said to reflect the three protagonists' shattered sense of self. This link is particulary strong in a sequence where the familiar auditory sliding from the stories of the vice-consul and Anne-Marie Stretter to the beggarwoman's chant is accompanied by three different shots of broken mirrors and windows. Many of these recurring images, then, can be seen as metaphors for what is suggested by the voices. Hence, whereas in *India Song* the images are still recognisable as representa-tions of the protagonists, in *Son nom de Venise* they evoke generalised states of being rather than specific individuals. This can be illustrated by comparing a sequence in both films where we see two radically different images against the background of an identical section on the soundtrack. In this sequence, voice 2 comments that Anne-Marie Stretter is no longer suffering, since she is afflicted by 'leprosy of the heart'.[22] Whereas in *India Song* this verbal metaphor is accompanied by a long fixed shot of Delphine Seyrig, in *Son nom de Venise* the camera pans along large stone slabs, wrapped in plastic sheets and covered in green moss, creating a powerful image of Anne-Marie Stretter's physical and emotional disintegration. However, since the heroine of *India Song* is now absent from the screen, the image becomes depersonalised and, as such, acquires a broader significance in terms of collective rather than merely individual experience.

Despite the prominence in *Son nom de Venise* of metaphorical shots which suggest a relationship of similarity between spoken text and image, there are nevertheless a number of sequences where meta-phorical readings would not be appropriate. For, in those instances,

22 See the previous discussion of this section of India Song on p. 35.

the relationship between words and images is based on opposition and incongruence rather than on resemblance. The rhetorical figure of the oxymoron, which refers to the co-presence of opposites, represents a key feature of Duras's literary as well as of her filmic style and appears at various points in *Son nom de Venise*. Thus, for instance, the joyful dance music contrasts painfully with the obsessive imagery of death and decay suggested by the film's location.[23] Similarly, towards the end of the film, Duras creates an almost unbearable tension between the Vice-consul's scream, on the one hand, and the exuberance of the rumba paired with gentle panoramic shots of the park, the trees and the lake, on the other.[24] In another paradoxical sequence of this kind we see images of a dilapidated fireplace, while one of the voices exclaims in exulted tones: 'Que d'amour ce bal, que de désir'.[25] Although for Duras the tension between opposites was an inescapable part of human experience, their conjunction, through the stylistic figures of paradox and oxymoron, indicates that, in her work at least, she sought to resolve such conflict. In *Son nom de Venise* the ultimate synthesis lies in the transcendence of meaning itself, accomplished by some exquisite shots of alternating light and shadow, of the red and purple sky above the park and of the beggarwoman's sunset in the final scene. These images, like the theme tune of *India Song*, are not tied to any specific meaning, since they function primarily at an aesthetic and affective level. They transgress the symbolic order of abstract categories and definitions and thereby challenge the dominant role of the filmic image as a semantic vehicle.

Having stripped away the last vestiges of representational realism, *Son nom de Venise* uncovers another, less accessible level of experience. In *Le Cimetière anglais*, Duras's cameraman Bruno Nuytten described this process in the following terms: 'La caméra c'était comme un explorateur de l'inconscient d'une histoire qu'on avait déjà racontée'[26]

---

23 Whereas, for *India Song* Duras only used the exterior of the palace, in *Son nom de Venise* she filmed its crumbling interior as well, suggesting in this way that the colonial splendour of *India Song* has disintegrated and that, like its filmic location, the French embassy at Calcutta is now an abandoned ruin.

24 I am using 'panoramic shot' here to render the French term 'un panoramique' which is a very common device in Durassian cinema. It is usually a medium shot and it describes a gentle sweeping movement of the camera.

25 'How much love there was at the ball, how much desire.''

26 'The camera was like an explorer of the unconscious layer of a story that had already been told.''

(Duras and Noguez 1984b). If, in *India Song*, the camera still observes and records the external existence of people and objects, in *Son nom de Venise* it sheds light on the inner landscape of the unconscious, both that of the protagonists from the previous film and that of the spectator. This is expressed, for example, in a long sequence in which the camera, and with it the spectator's gaze, follows a torch as it slowly lights up and examines the dark corners of the cellar underneath the palace. These images coincide with Michael Lonsdale's voiceover speaking of the vice-consul's longing for love, condensed in the melody of *India Song*, and of his inability to experience such love: 'Je suis venu aux Indes à cause d'*India Song*. Cet air me donne envie d'aimer. Je n'ai jamais aimé'.[27] The soundtrack implicitly relates the camera's exploration of the cellar as an image of the unconscious to the vice-consul's repressed desire which finally explodes into his cry of anguish, as he begs Anne-Marie Stretter to let him stay with her, if only for one night. In *Son nom de Venise*, then, by destroying the opulent images of *India Song*, Duras also destroys our conscious visual memory. Instead, the second film, with its stark archaic imagery, reactivates the primal unconscious layers of memory and creates what Ropars-Wuilleumier has described as 'un jeu d'échos et de traces'[28] (Ropars-Wuilleumier 1979: 7).

As Borgomano has argued, the conspicuous absence of human figures and the destruction of material objects in *Son nom de Venise* proclaims the impermanence and hence the vanity of all things (Borgomano 1985: 130). While I agree with this interpretation, I would also suggest that this aspect of the film has another purpose, to the extent that the absence of the protagonists and the empty quality of the images emphasise the soundtrack more strongly than in *India Song*. The image-track of the second film, with its lack of representation, works even more powerfully as a contrasting device, enhancing the soundtrack and giving it an uncanny resonance. The importance of sound in this film is even implicit in its title which foregrounds not only the sonorous quality of the Italian name but also Venice as the place which invokes Anne-Marie Stretter's love of music. If the external world, represented by images, has come to an end in *Son nom de Venise*, the film's soundtrack reconnects spectators to the inner reality

27 'I came to India because of *India Song*. This tune makes me want to love. I've never loved.'

28 'a play of echoes and traces'

of their own memory, desire and imagination. To illustrate this point, it is worth recalling one of the central scenes of *India Song* where Anne-Marie Stretter dances with the young attaché in front of a large mirror. During this section of the film, the spectator's attention is so absorbed by the two figures, their movements and their mirror images, that the voices on the soundtrack recede into the background. In *Son nom de Venise*, on the other hand, this sequence has been replaced by a long fixed frame showing an empty room. It is against the backdrop of this visual void that we are able to focus more clearly on the off-screen voices and, in particular, on the conversation between Anne-Marie Stretter and her dancing partner, as she talks about her indifference to life, her stifled musical creativity, Venice, her lost desire. The emotional resonance of what is being said is stronger here, where the voices are projected into an empty room, than in *India Song* where they are overshadowed by the on-screen figures, in particular that of Anne-Marie Stretter. While it is likely that the spectator of *India Song* associates the fictional woman with the visual presence of Delphine Seyrig, in *Son nom de Venise* this link is broken through the protagonist's absence from the screen. The name of Anne-Marie Stretter, uttered by the female voices, has thus become an empty signifier which may ultimately represent the experience of desire and alienation in general, but which is no longer embodied by a specific woman. The slow process of destruction, reflected in the long fixed frames of *India Song* is followed by a sense of liberation in *Son nom de Venise*. For, in this film, the music is in tune with the continuous displacement of the camera, as it travels across the park, along the outside walls of the house and through its empty rooms. In fact, according to Ropars-Wuilleumier, out of the seventy-eight shots that make up the entire film, the majority are either tracking or 'panoramic' shots (Ropars-Wuilleumier 1979: 11). The fluid quality of this film indicates that, although death and destruction are certainly implicit in the images themselves, both the rhythm of the music and the camera's mobility finally release the repressed desire of *India Song*.

Le Navire Night

'Chaque être est distinct de tous les autres [...] Lui seul naît. Lui seul meurt. Entre un être et un autre, il y a un abîme, il y a une discontinuité'[29] (Bataille 1964: 35). This quotation from *L'Erotisme* by Georges Bataille, whose work Duras greatly admired, encapsulates the essence of *Le Navire Night*, one of her lesser known but most powerful and magical films. The soundtrack records the voices of Duras herself and of the filmmaker Benoît Jacquot reading the text of *Le Navire Night* which tells the following story: a young man, identified only by the initials J. M. and who works for a telecommunications company, dials a number at random and is connected to a woman's voice. This is the beginning of a three-year love affair conducted entirely by telephone, since the relationship can only survive on condition that the lovers never actually meet. Although we know little about the man, a fairly detailed picture of the woman emerges from the telephone conversations: known to J. M. as F., she is 26 years old, a medical student and the illegitimate daughter of a rich and powerful man. She suffers from leukaemia and, just before her death, she marries her doctor. This story is framed by brief narrative fragments about Duras's impressions of a visit to Athens, as she remembers the deadly, frightening silence which rises with the midday sun, the sense of loneliness and the absence of love which the couple in 'the other story' are attempting to overcome. As we listen to the voices, the image-track presents us with shots of the sixteenth arrondissement of Paris, in particular the quartier de la Défense, the park surrounding the Musée Galliera, the Bois de Boulogne, as well as of the Seine and the Père Lachaise cemetery. Several sequences are filmed inside a villa and feature three well-known actors: Bulle Ogier, Dominique Sanda and Mathieu Carrière who had already appeared in *India Song*. While the story of *Le Navire Night* is rather stereotyped, as Borgomano has pointed out (Borgomano 1985: 148), Duras's film avoids falling into melodrama precisely by not representing either the narrative or the characters themselves. Instead, *Le Navire Night*, both as text and film, distils the essence of how people may experience loneliness, separateness and the desire to reach out across the 'abyss' mentioned by Bataille.

What is important here is Duras's notion of desire as an end in itself. For her protagonists the experience of waiting and longing for fulfilment becomes more important than fulfilment itself, since the latter is always short-lived and, by definition, spells the end of desire.

---

29 'Each being is distinct from all the others [...] He is born alone. He dies alone. Between one being and another, there is an abyss, there is a discontinuity.'

It follows, then, that desire can only be sustained by constantly postponing its satisfaction. In *Le Navire Night* this idea is taken to its logical conclusion, since the two lovers deliberately avoid meeting each other, so that their mutual passion arises entirely from the mental images they create of each other during their telephone conversations: 'Sans fin se décrivent. L'un l'autre. A l'un, l'autre'[30] (Duras 1979: 26). So, desire is closely allied with the projection of certain fantasies on to another person whose very absence guarantees the survival of the fantasy and hence of desire itself. According to this model, then, the image of the other emanates from and is a part of the self which creates it. Hence, in *Le Navire Night*, the lovers' identities merge into one, as the distinctions between subject and object disappear: 'Je me regarde avec tes yeux'[31] (Duras 1979: 27). Similarly, conventional temporal and spatial categories are fused together, as the lovers' story seems suspended in eternity: 'Il dit avoir confondu les moments, les jours, les lieux, ne pas avoir de chronologie'[32] (Duras 1979: 87). Even sexual identities become uncertain, since the ambiguous use of masculine and feminine pronouns in the text creates some confusion between the male and the female character (Duras 1979: 87). This textual pattern of ambiguity is reflected, moreover, in the film's use of disembodied voices and bodiless images. As in other works by Duras, such a blurring of distinctions is motivated by the desire to overcome the painful, yet inevitable distance that separates people from each other. The vessel of the film's title stands for this movement of desire as it crosses the metaphorical sea of loneliness, representing Paris at night: 'Ce territoire de Paris la nuit, insomniaque, c'est la mer sur laquelle passe le Night [...] Les mouvements du Navire Night devraient témoigner des mouvements du désir'[33] (Duras 1979: 37). But since the man's love for the woman depends on her absence, to see her would destroy the relationship. Therefore, when F. sends two photographs of herself to J. M., the movement of desire suddenly ceases, as the vessel is stopped in its flow: 'L'histoire s'arrête

30 'They describe themselves endlessly. Each other. To each other.'
31 'I look at myself with your eyes.'
32 'He says that he got the moments mixed up, the days and the places, that he had no chronology.'
33 'The sleepless territory of Paris at night is the sea on which the Night glides past. [...] The movement of the Navire Night should bear witness to the movement of desire.'

avec les photographies [...] Le désir est mort, tué par une image'[34] (Duras 1979: 51–2). This indictment of the image may equally well be applied to the cinema as a whole, since for Duras, as we have seen, visual representation limits or even destroys the imagination and hence the source of desire itself.

Given this rejection of representation, it is not surprising that there are no apparent links between the soundtrack and the image-track of *Le Navire Night*. Despite the occasional parallels, such as shots of the river at night and of the park mentioned in the text, the story told by the voices and the images we see on the screen function independently of each other. What does, however, hold the two parts of the film together is the compelling quality of both the images and of the voices that draw the spectator into the experience of the prota-gonists evoked in the text. The form of the film itself, then, recreates its own subject matter, as the spectator enters into the transitional space between text and image, where our rational analytical mind temporarily gives way to that sense of fascination which Duras described as being part of desire (Duras 1996: 93). This blank space which is occasionally suggested by the use of the black screen in the film might also relate to 'l'image noire', the 'black image' in the text on to which J. M. projects his visions of F. (Duras 1979: 87). In the same way as J. M. produces his own image of the woman, the film itself reflects whatever the spectator may project on to it. This reflexive quality of the film is implicit in several stunning visual sequences. The second opening shot, for instance, shows the mirror image of a park and a lake which, in a kind of double mirror effect, reflects the shimmering surface of the water. The merging in the film of time, space and identities is emphasised, furthermore, by the circularity of the image-track, as the closing sections feature the same shots Duras had already used immediately after the credit sequence at the beginning of the film.

In the prologue of the text Duras explains that, after only two days of shooting, she was on the verge of abandoning *Le Navire Night*, but then decided instead to film the process of filming itself, or as she put it,'tourner le désastre du film'[35] (Duras 1979: 15). This meant that some of the technical devices and procedures used during the shoot-ing of a film, but which are normally invisible in the final product,

34 'The story ends with the photographs [...] Desire is dead, killed by an image.'
35 'shoot the disaster of the film'

actually appear in several images and sequences: projectors, screens, lighting all remind us that we are watching a film, after all, and thereby distance us to some extent from the hypnotic effect it otherwise exerts on the spectator. The participation of the three actors who cannot, in any way, be assimilated to the characters of Duras's text provides a clear example of this distancing device which becomes particularly effective during three sequences showing a make-up artist preparing the actors for their appearance in front of the camera. In *Le Navire Night* the obvious differentiation between actors and protagonists also highlights the uncertainties surrounding the protagonists' 'true' identities, in particular that of F. who provides contradictory self-descriptions at various points in the text. These ambiguities are reflected in the physical differences between Bulle Ogier and Dominique Sanda, both of whom might play the part of the elusive F. By drawing attention to its own making, then, the film reveals itself as a product, an artificial construct, like the actresses' meticulously made-up faces. But more importantly perhaps, instead of making a narrative film which would have provided a 'realistic' representation of her story, with *Le Navire Night* Duras questions the very distinctions between the appearances of external reality and the inner world of the imagination.

Césarée

The short film *Césarée* was released in November 1979, along with *Les Mains négatives*, *Aurélia Steiner (Melbourne)* and *Aurélia Steiner (Vancouver)*. All four works are accompanied by written texts, read by Duras herself who provides the only voiceover on the soundtracks. *Césarée* was shot in July 1979 in two familiar Parisian locations: the virtually deserted Jardins des Tuileries were filmed at 8 a.m. and the Place de la Concorde during the afternoon of the same day. The film evokes the ruins of the ancient Jewish city of Cesarea, on the northwest coast of Israel, which had existed from 13 BC until its destruction in AD 1265. On a journey through Israel, Duras visited the site of the former city and, enchanted by it, deliberately missed her plane in order to return to Cesarea (Duras and Noguez 1984c). For Duras, the place has since become synonymous with Berenice, the last Queen of the Jews and heroine of Racine's tragedy *Bérénice*, which directly inspired the film. The historical Berenice, born in AD 28, supported

the Romans during the Jewish war, when she became the lover of the
Emperor Vespasian's son Titus, the commander of Judea who destroyed
the temple of Jerusalem. She later went into voluntary exile when she
joined Titus in Rome, but was rejected by him for political reasons, as
he himself became emperor and unwillingly succumbed to pressure
from the Senate to end his relationship with Berenice, because of her
origins and lower social status. In Duras's version of the story,
Berenice leaves Rome and returns to Cesarea, devastated by the pain
of rejection and enforced separation: 'Arrachée à lui/ Au désir de lui/
En meurt'[36] (Duras 1979: 101).

Although based on historical events, the film is detached from its
factual anchorage in time and space, as Cesarea is transported from
antiquity to late twentieth-century Paris. Like the story of Berenice,
Cesarea becomes a pretext for the projection of familiar Durassian
preoccupations, crystallising the inevitable conjunction in her work of
desire, exile and separation. Despite obvious differences in terms of
the protagonists, settings and events, *Césarée* is reminiscent of *Son
nom de Venise*, in so far as Berenice, like Anne-Marie Stretter before
her, embodies the recurring thematic patterns that inhabit Duras's
texts and films. In this sense, if *Son nom de Venise* announces the
physical death of Anne-Marie Stretter, *Césarée* represents her resurrection through Berenice. This connection between the two films is
underscored, moreover, by the absence of human figuration and the
sense of emptiness and desolation that characterises Duras's visual
style in both works. However, whereas in *Son nom de Venise* Anne-
Marie Stretter's existence is still invoked through her name, the figure
of Berenice in *Césarée* is elided, both verbally and visually, as the
female protagonist, in a metonymic shift typical of Duras, merges
with the city with which she is associated. The absence of Berenice
highlights the emotional and physical devastation which, for many of
Duras's heroines, is equivalent to the destruction of their identity.
Anonymous and faceless, like the beggarwoman in previous films,
Berenice is stripped of her proper name and even of the female pro-
noun 'elle' whose frequent omission in the text further emphasises
her loss of self: 'Muette, blanche comme la craie, apparaît./Sans honte
aucune'[37] (Duras 1979: 101). Emptied of her individuality, she becomes
an archetypal female figure, ubiquitous and ageless, whose anguish

36 'Torn away from him./ From her desire for him./She is dying.'
37 'Speechless, as white as chalk, appears./Without any shame.'

transcends personal boundaries and spills over into the world: 'La nouvelle de la douleur éclate et se/répand sur le monde [...] Elle était très jeune, dix-huit ans, trente/ans, deux mille ans'[38] (Duras 1979: 100–1).

The timeless and universal quality of Berenice's story is reflected in the opening sequences of the film, which focus on a series of female bronze statues by Aristide Maillol (1861–1944).[39] As the camera gently circles the first statue, looking at it from different angles, Duras reads the first two stanzas of the text *Césarée*. Through the repeated incantation of the word 'Cesarea', the place becomes synonymous not only with the historical figure of Berenice, but also with Maillol's statue whose posture of desperate isolation seems to embody the narrative of love, betrayal and abandonment read by Duras. In the film the underlying relationship between text and image brings together the different dimensions of time, space and identity, as the ruins of Cesarea are resurrected in the centre of Paris and the story of Berenice is projected on to Maillol's sculptures. Duras's use of tracking shots during the Maillol sequences is a reflection of this sliding from past to present, from the individual to the universal which underpins the film's structural framework. In another sense, the movement described by the tracking shots also signifies the theme of the journey and of exile, as Berenice, impelled by her desire, renounces her position as Queen, her home, her origins and embarks on the long voyage to Rome, only to return to Cesarea after she has been abandoned by her lover.[40] The beginning and the end of the woman's story, then, are marked by a journey which corresponds to the opening and closing sections of the film, where the camera glides along the Jardins des Tuileries and the walls of the Louvre. The relationship between text and image is particularly striking, furthermore, in a sequence towards the end of the film where the section in the text relating Berenice's return voyage to Cesarea is directly linked to the image-track, as the camera travels along the Seine in a slow funereal

38 'The news of her sorrow breaks and/spreads all over the world [...] She was very young, 18, 30,/2,000 years old.'

39 That the statues themselves represent emotional states rather than specific women is implicit in their titles, such as *La Douleur* (1922).

40 Paradoxically, the French term for the tracking shot, 'le travelling', reflects much more clearly the relationship between subject matter and camerawork in Duras's films than its English equivalent.

movement. But these images of the river represent more than a visual support for the story of Berenice, since the element of water in Duras, whether represented by the river or by the sea, has a more general and ambiguous significance. For if, on the one hand, water symbolises the dynamic energy of desire which compels the protagonists in Duras's fiction and films to pursue an unattainable ideal of happiness, on the other hand, it also embodies the destructiveness of such desire, the intensity of which threatens to engulf and drown the individual. But, as in *Césarée*, it is typically a female figure who has the courage to follow her desire to the end, despite the threat of madness, social exclusion and even death. Titus, on the other hand, chooses to sacrifice his feelings to political power and thus to the values of the patriarchal order, represented by the state.

Following the opening sequence of *Césarée*, tracking shots alternate with long fixed frames showing a second statue which is situated in the Place de la Concorde. The camera's oscillation between these two sets of images underpins the structure of the film which is built around the opposition between desire and movement, on the one hand, and immobility, stagnation and death, on the other. The second statue, with its crown and its majestic presence, might suggest a more literal and easily identifiable embodiment of Berenice than the bronze figures in the park, particularly when Duras's voice tells the story of the queen's exile, repudiation and expulsion from Rome (Duras 1979: 97, 99), while the camera lingers on the statue's face, eroded by time and by the elements. However, the alternation between these fixed images and the tracking shots of Maillol's work, which becomes more frequent towards the end of the film, suggests a strong identification between 'Berenice' and the other female sculptures. This sliding from the individual to the transpersonal is also implicit in several back-lit shots of the statue, showing its silhouette in contrast with the blue sky. These shots, focusing only on the blurred outlines of the figure draw attention to its anonymous status, as Berenice's private suffering is universalised: 'Douleur./L'intolérable./La douleur de leur séparation'[41] (Duras 1979: 96). The sense of isolation and entrapment emanating from the statue is expressed by the visual metaphor of the scaffolding and the black canvasses that evoke the image of Berenice on the Roman vessel, imprisoned by grief (Duras 1979: 100). At the

41 'Sorrow./The unbearable./The sorrow of their separation.'

same time, of course, just as the statue was being repaired during the shooting of *Césarée*, the film itself, as well as Duras's text, resurrect the story of Berenice.

The survival and preservation of memory is a central concern in Duras's work. In *Césarée* this preoccupation with the memory of Berenice and of Cesarea is reflected in a fairly brief section of the image-track, showing close-up shots of the obelisk in the Place de la Concorde. The hieroglyphics on the stone slabs evoke ancient histories and civilisations which are implicitly related to the people of Cesarea, as we listen to Duras reading the corresponding text: 'Dans cette poussière/on voit encore, on lit encore la pensée/des gens de Césarée/ le tracé des rues des peuples de Césarée'[42] (Duras 1979: 99). The choice of the obelisk is significant here in two ways. First, because of its solidity and durability, stone becomes a metaphor for the preservation of memory, whether in the form of statues or of the obelisk, which literally contains records written in stone. Second, the hieroglyphics, composed of symbols and pictures, are significant in so far as they mirror the close relationship between text and image which characterises Duras's cinema itself. However, although in *Césarée* there is a more direct semantic correlation between the soundtrack and the visual track than in some of Duras's other films, the importance of the text nevertheless outweighs that of the image. The visual minimalism typical of Duras is emphasised here by the use of the black screen, as the empty frame alludes to the ephemeral nature of the visible and the visual realm. For what ultimately survives destruction and death in Duras's world is not the image, but the written and the spoken word that are alone capable of preserving memory: 'Il n'en reste que la mémoire de l'histoire/et ce seul mot pour la nommer/ Césarée/La totalité./Rien que l'endroit/Et le mot'[43] (Duras 1979: 95). The centrality of words is highlighted, furthermore, by the fact that the text of *Césarée* is like a poem, structured around the repetition of keywords and emphasising the sonorous and rhythmical quality of language. *Césarée* was the first film by Duras where the text was read entirely by the director herself. It is not surprising that this exclusive use of the female voice appears in a film whose central figure is also

42 'In the dust/you can still see, read the thoughts/of the people of Cesarea/the outline of the streets of the people of Cesarea.'
43 'All that is left is the memory of the story/and this one word to name it/Cesarea/ Everything/Only the place/And the word.'

female, suggesting that Duras identified to some extent with her heroine. More importantly perhaps, if Berenice's destruction stems directly from her lover's subordination to the patriarchal order of the Roman State, the film and the text seem to vindicate finally the power of the female voice, condensed in Duras's incantation of Cesarea.

Aurélia Steiner (Melbourne)

This film and its sequel *Aurélia Steiner (Vancouver)*, both made in 1979, trace a young Jewish woman's search for her identity and her origins, as she attempts to reconnect with her parents who died in a concentration camp. Although the memory of the Holocaust becomes central to the second film, in *Aurélia Melbourne*[44] it remains implicit in a few textual references, while the main focus is on the woman's desire to communicate, through her letters, with a nameless male figure, referred to throughout the text as 'you'. Like the recipient of the letters, their author remains anonymous since the writing 'I' does not identify herself as Aurélia Steiner until the end of the film. Text and film suggest the terrible isolation of the young woman who needs to establish a dialogue with the unknown 'you', so that she may confirm her identity through his. Instead of individual self-expression, writing becomes a way of calling out to a distant 'other', an act of love through which Aurélia hopes to overcome the abyss of time that separates her from him: 'Comment nous faire nous rapprocher ensemble de cet amour, annuler cette apparente fragmentation des temps qui nous séparent l'un de l'autre?'[45] (Duras 1979: 118). The constant repetition of the imperative 'écoutez ' – 'listen' – implies that writing is also a vocal and verbal form of communication, similar to the telephone conversations in *Le Navire Night*. Yet, unlike J. M. in the previous film, the male interlocutor in *Aurélia Melbourne* remains silent. While repeated references in the text suggest that he may have died in a concentration camp, (Duras 1979: 120, 127, 130), it is not until *Aurélia Vancouver* that Duras confirms that the addressee of Aurélia's letters is indeed her father who was hanged at Auschwitz, because he had

---

44 Following Duras's own suggestion, I shall refer to the two Aurélia Steiner films as *Aurélia Melbourne* and *Aurélia Vancouver* respectively (Duras 1979: 17).

45 'How can I make us draw closer to this love together, how can I cancel the apparent fragmentation of time which separates us from each other?'

'stolen' some soup to feed his child (Duras 1979: 158). In both texts the father's life is recreated through the letters, so that writing becomes invested with the power to transcend death: 'lorsque je vous écris personne n'est mort'.[46] But although *Aurélia Melbourne* needs to be read against its specific historical background, the text and the film nevertheless remain an integral part of the constellation of themes and characters which define Duras's fictional world as a whole. This connection becomes evident when we look at the complex image of the starving white cat who is implicitly identified with Aurélia Steiner. Like her, the cat is abandoned, as his physical starvation parallels the woman's emotional deprivation and exile. The repeated verbal association between the cat and leprosy, furthermore, connects *Aurélia Melbourne* with *India Song*, as we are reminded of Calcutta and the starving beggarwoman from Savannakhet (Duras 1979: 122, 124). Similarly, the theme of exile links Aurélia Steiner not only to Anne-Marie Stretter but ultimately also to Marguerite Duras herself. At the end of the film it is only when the cat dies that Aurélia is symbolically reunited with her father and seems finally able to embrace her identity by naming herself: 'Je m'appelle Aurélia Steiner./Je vis à Melbourne où mes parents sont professeurs./J'ai dix-huit ans./J'écris'[47] (Duras 1979: 135). It is as if the cat's death, brought about partly by Aurélia's refusal to feed him, represents an almost deliberate sacrifice which, in a reversal of events, finally allows her to come to terms with her father's death, since he had sacrificed his own life to save her from starvation in the camp.

At first glance the semantic discontinuity between text and image may appear more abrupt and violent in *Aurélia Melbourne* than in Duras's previous films. For while the words on the soundtrack recall two thousand years of violence and suffering, the spectators' gaze is gently carried along by the camera as it travels slowly down the river Seine, taking us past the lights shimmering on the water, the play of light and darkness under the bridges and finally resting on the

---

46 'when I'm writing to you nobody has died.' From an autobiographical perspective, this sentence echoes Duras's comment in' *Les Yeux verts* that, while working on *Aurélia Steiner*, she was going through a difficult stage in her life and that writing was her means of survival: 'Quand j'écris je ne meurs pas' – 'When I'm writing I'm not dying' (Duras 1996: 12).

47 'My name is Aurélia Steiner. I live in Melbourne where my parents are teachers. I'm 18 years old. I write.'

reflections of six street lamps glistening on the blue and violet surface of the river. Taken in a literal sense, the serene beauty of these shots clashes with the sense of desolation and anguish that emanates from the text. However, as in *Son nom de Venise dans Calcutta désert*, it is precisely the discrepancy between words and images that makes the former resonate all the more powerfully. The significance of the words is heightened by the soothing quality of the single tracking sequence along the river that allows the spectator to disengage from the usual distractions of the visual imagination and to enter instead into the space off-screen where we hear Duras's voice recite the text. The image, rather than swallowing up words and sounds, gives them back their full force, both in terms of their meaning and the musical quality characteristic of Duras's writing.

Despite this striking use of desynchronisation, the two parts of the film are nevertheless linked by an underlying relationship between its images and the pattern of themes and motifs implicit in the text. As in *Césarée*, the tracking shots of the river suggest the theme of the journey, as Aurélia travels through history and memory. However, the continuous movement of the river, like that of the camera, dissolves individual identities, since the figure of Aurélia Steiner, despite the different cities and continents with which she is associated in the two films, embodies the same woman. For Duras, she represents all the survivors of the Holocaust, the second generation of Jewish refugees who may have been born in Melbourne or Vancouver and who perhaps never returned to Europe: 'Elle est encore rue des Rosiers, d'abord là, puis ailleurs en même temps, toujours là, puis toujours ailleurs ensuite, ici comme ailleurs, dans tous les juifs, la première génération c'est elle, comme la dernière'[48] (Duras 1996: 125). This blurring of boundaries is reflected not only in the liquidity of the images of *Aurélia Melbourne*, but also in the flowing quality of the words we hear on the soundtrack. In this sense, the film's visual track is a metaphor for the text itself and for what Duras later called *l'écriture courante* to describe the fluid style of writing she developed in *L'Amant* (1984). Indeed, the river in *Aurélia Melbourne* recalls the powerful image of the Mekong in *L'Amant* and thus represents what

48 'She is still in the rue des Rosiers, first there, then elsewhere at the same time, always there, then always elsewhere, here as elsewhere, in all Jews, she is the first generation and the last.' (The rue des Rosiers is a street in the Jewish quarter of Paris.)

Duras has called 'une image passe-partout' (Duras 1996: 76), an empty, all-purpose image that might signifiy the Seine, the Mekong or even the Ganges mentioned in *India Song* and that functions like a mirror reflecting key motifs from her other texts and films.

In the work of Duras, water imagery generally retains its traditional mythological significance as a feminine element, associated in particular with the figure of the mother. As Nathalie Heinrich has argued, the river in *Aurélia Melbourne* facilitates the spectator's regression towards an archaic maternal space, as the film's image-track lulls us into a trance-like state, generating an increased receptiveness in the spectator to the soothing quality of Duras's language and of her voice (Heinrich 1980: 46). The pervasive presence of water in this film would also suggest that the overt search for Aurélia's father is accompanied by a more implicit longing to be reunited with the mother whose loss is recovered symbolically by the gentle flow of the river. If the dislocation between words and images is analogous to the separation between 'I' and 'you' in the text, the fluidity of the image-track corresponds to the desire to overcome this distance through an imaginary merging of 'self' and 'other'.

Aurélia Steiner (Vancouver)

The hypnotic effect of *Aurélia Melbourne* is replaced in its sequel by a stark black and white image-track, as the film's central preoccupation is with the Holocaust and, in particular, with Aurélia's reliving of the events surrounding her birth which coincided with her parents' death. As Duras has indicated, this film is partly based on events described by Elie Wiesel in *La Nuit* (Wiesel 1958), the testimony of his experience of Auschwitz (Duras 1996: 143). In his book, Wiesel recalls the agony of a 13-year-old Jewish boy who was hanged for having taken some soup. Because he was so emaciated, the boy struggled for three days and three nights at the end of the rope before he finally died. In *Aurélia Vancouver* Duras translated the intolerable memory of the child's suffering into her own narrative of the father's death in the main yard of the camp, represented by the haunting image of 'the white rectangle of death' (Duras 1979: 156). In Duras's text and film, Aurélia's mother also dies, having given birth to her child in the barracks of Auschwitz.

Although still in the form of a letter to the father, the first-person narrative which constitutes the soundtrack of *Aurélia Vancouver* constructs more directly Aurélia's relationship with both parents. Through a complex interplay of identifications and fusional experiences she gradually overcomes her sense of alienation and inner emptiness, as she begins to develop her own subjectivity by incorporating the images of her parents that she creates through her writing and which, in *Aurélia Melbourne*, were either uncertain or absent. Thus, her relationship with the hitherto anonymous addressee of the letters is stated in the opening sections of the text: 'Je m'appelle Aurélia Steiner. Je suis votre enfant'[49] (Duras 1979: 142). This initial declaration of 'self' in terms of the name and the familial link is gradually strengthened as Aurélia continues to create herself through her physical similarity with her father and, more crucially perhaps, through her relationship with her mother. Throughout the text her mental image of the father remains fixed at the time of his death, at 18, and is subsequently displaced on to other men, young sailors with whom Aurélia has brief sexual encounters: 'Parfois d'autres viennent. Ils ont quelquefois l'âge que vous auriez eu. Dans un monde où vous n'êtes pas en vie ils peuvent me tenir lieu de notre rencontre'[50] (Duras 1979: 143). Considering that the imaginary father is the same age as Aurélia herself and that there is a strong resemblance between them (Duras 1979: 143), it is conceivable that he represents not so much the paternal image as the more familiar Durassian figure of the 'twin' brother, which recurs in the later film *Agatha*. Although Aurélia's fantasies do have incestuous overtones, as Bernard Alazet has suggested (Alazet 1982: 58), her sexual desire is inseparable from her need for self-recognition in and by another, be it the imaginary father, the brother or the anonymous sailors. But of equal significance here is the mother who has remained absent from *Aurélia Melbourne*, a silence which may be explained by the grief, and possibly guilt, associated with her memory, since her death in the camp coincided with Aurélia's birth. In the second film-text these repressed feelings are gradually released through writing, as Aurélia describes the final moments of her mother's life: 'Vous voyiez encore, je crois, mais déjà vous ne souffriez plus, déjà atteinte d'insensibilité. Vous baigniez

49 'My name is Aurélia Steiner. I'm your child.'
50 'Sometimes others come. Sometimes they are the same age you would have been. In a world where you're not alive they can replace our encounter.'

dans le sang de ma naissance. Je reposais à vos côtés dans la poussière du sol'[51] (Duras 1979: 149). This imaginary recreation of the mother coincides with the recurring poetic evocation of the sea, which serves as a leitmotif both in the text and on the film's image-track. In the work of Duras the image of the sea is generally associated with the archetypal figure of the mother, a link that is strengthened by the homophonic relationship in French between 'la mer' (the sea) and 'la mère' (the mother). This ambiguity is clearly conveyed by Duras's recitation of her text on the soundtrack of *Aurélia Vancouver*, where the two words and hence their respective meanings and connotations are fused together. Numerous descriptions of the sea in human terms, furthermore, reinforce its status as a metaphor for the mother's body. This personification is particularly striking in several passages where Aurélia's wish to be reunited with her mother is expressed in terms of her physical immersion in and identification with the sea, as the latter comes to represent both her mother and herself: 'Je suis allée me coucher sur la profondeur de la mer, face au ciel glacé. Elle était encore fiévreuse, chaude./Petite fille. Amour. Petite enfant./Je l'ai appelée de noms divers, de celui d'Aurélia, d'Aurélia Steiner'[52] (Duras 1979: 154–5). In this passage Aurélia's fusion with the depths of the ocean might suggest a temporary return to the womb, where the imaginary merging between mother and daughter expresses itself in terms of a reversal of roles where the sea/the mother becomes the little girl, Aurélia Steiner. But it is only through this physical and verbal intimacy with the mother that Aurélia is able to re-emerge from the ocean, a rebirth which finally allows her to declare her subjectivity. In the concluding episode of the text, at Aurélia's own instigation, the sailor/father names her and thus confirms both her personal and her collective Jewish identity: 'Il dit: Juden, Juden Aurélia, Juden Aurélia Steiner'[53] (Duras 1979: 164). It is worth noting here that Duras deliberately chose the German word 'Juden', used by the Nazis as an insult, and transformed it into a term of self-affirmation, as Aurélia's reunion with both parents now establishes her identity and history.

51 'You could still see, I think, but already you were no longer suffering, you could no longer feel anything. You were lying in the blood of my birth. I was sleeping next to you on the dusty floor.'

52 'I lay down on the depths of the sea, facing the icy sky. It was still feverish, hot./ Little girl. Love. Little child./I called it by different names, that of Aurélia, Aurélia Steiner.'

53 'He says: Jews, Jews Aurélia, Jews Aurélia Steiner.'

The semantic relationship between soundtrack and image-track is perhaps more apparent in *Aurélia Vancouver* than in previous films, particularly as the condensed textual image of the mother and the sea is easily recognisable in the recurring oceanic images of waves, rocks and beaches. There is a profound distinction in this film, however, between the descriptive and visually evocative text and the image-track, composed of a few black and white shots of sea and landscapes which are repeated at significant points in the film. To the richness of the verbal image, then, corresponds the relative emptiness of the visual image. In *Aurélia Vancouver* this lack of visual representation has a particularly powerful effect on the viewer, since we are unable to externalise and thereby distance ourselves from the events described by projecting them on to the cinema screen. On the contrary, when we 'see' Duras's film, instead of looking at images in front of us, we need to create our own internal vision. By their very absence from the visual track of the film, the textual images describing, for example, 'the white rectangle of death' are intensified, as they resonate within the viewer and thus become part of her or his inner experience. *Aurélia Vancouver* clearly demonstrates the limitations of cinema, as the horror of Auschwitz is beyond representation.

The film's visual rhythm is sustained by alternating images of the sea and rocks, on the one hand, and shots of a rural landscape, on the other hand. These images of summer skies, the open countryside and rows of tall, slender trees recur at regular intervals to coincide with specific sections on the soundtrack where Duras reads the scenes relating to the death of Aurélia's parents: 'Autour de vous, dure et craquée de soleil, cette terre étrangère, cette lumière, cet été parfait, ce ciel de chaleur'[54] (Duras 1979: 149). The images suggest the desolate, remote countryside around Auschwitz, as Duras commented in *Les Yeux Verts*: 'Les camps de concentration allemands, Auschwitz, Birkenau étaient des lieux continentaux, étouffants, très froids en hiver, brûlants en été, très loin à l'intérieur de l'Europe, très loin de la mer'[55] (Duras 1996: 129). If these images evoke the physical surroundings of Auschwitz, the recurring metonymic shots of railway tracks and abandoned

---

54 'Around you, hard and cracked by the sun, is this foreign earth, this light, this perfect summer, this sky of heat.'

55 'The German concentration camps, Auschwitz, Birkenau were continental places, suffocating, very cold in winter and scorching in the summer, very far inland, inside Europe, very far from the sea.'

train stations recall the deportation to the camps. These sequences in *Aurélia Vancouver* are reminiscent of Claude Lanzmann's film *Shoah* (1985) in which interviews with survivors of the Holocaust alternate with images of the woods around Auschwitz and the railway tracks leading up to the main gates of the camp. But at the same time the contrast between land and sea in Duras's film may also be linked to the destruction of the land described in the text, when, during a violent storm, the sea assaults and devastates a town, possibly as an act of retribution, as Dominique Noguez has suggested: 'la mer agit pour punir les hommes du scandale des camps'[56] (Duras and Noguez 1984c).

The visual sequences in *Aurélia Vancouver*, as in previous films, derive their significance largely from the text. Emptied of their obvious literal meanings, these images function at the figurative level, as metaphoric or, more commonly, metonymic representations of the events and experiences described in the text. But in *Aurélia Vancouver* Duras has gone a step further towards undermining the dominance of the image in cinema by fusing text and image together into what she called 'l'image écrite', 'the written image' (Duras 1996: 142). The written image which shows words or even entire segments of text on the screen appears at several junctures in the film, where the name *Aurélia Steiner*, in Duras's handwriting, appears on the blank screen. This technique of 'writing on the image' takes on a special significance during the lovemaking ritual towards the end of the film, where the verbal repetition of the name is reflected in its graphic form on the screen. Ultimately it is the name and hence language itself which assures Aurélia of her identity as an integral part of Jewish history and memory.

In conclusion, then, the two *Aurélia Steiner* films are a landmark in Duras's work, in so far as they crystallise both the themes and filmic discourses characteristic of her production as a whole. But they distinguish themselves from films such as *India Song* by their explicitly historical perspective and, therefore, the broader political issues they raise. Central to these is the question of power, both in its social context and in relation to the cinema as a dominant medium of representation in contemporary Western cultures. The next chapter will explore the politics of cinema in Duras and show how her cinematographic technique is directly linked to her political concerns with feminism, communism and colonialism.

56 'the sea acts to punish mankind for the scandal of the camps'

References

Alazet, B. (1982), 'Je m'appelle Aurélia Steiner', *Didascalies*, 3: 51–60.

Bataille, G. (1964), *L'Erotisme*, Paris, UGE.

Bernheim, N. (1974), 'Autour d'un film – *India Song*', *Revue du cinéma*, 291: 38–60.

Borgomano, M. (1985), *L'Ecriture filmique de Marguerite Duras*, Paris, Albatros.

Bouquet, S. (1996), 'M. Duras: L'œuvre en miettes', *Cahiers du cinéma*, 501: 36–7.

Chion, M. (1993), *La Voix au cinéma*, Paris, Seuil.

Duras, M. (1973), *Nathalie Granger suivi de La Femme du Gange*, Paris, Gallimard.

Duras, M. (1977), *Le Cumion*, Paris, Minuit.

Duras, M. (1979), *Le Navire Night – Césarée – Les Mains négatives – Aurélia Steiner*, Paris, Mercure de France.

Duras, M. (1980), 'Notes on *India Song*', *Camera Obscura*, 6: 42–9.

Duras, M. (1984), *L'Amant*, Paris, Minuit.

Duras, M. (1996), *Les Yeux verts*, Paris, Editions de l'étoile/Cahiers du cinéma.

Duras, M. *et al.* (1979), *Marguerite Duras*, Paris, Albatros, Collection ça cinéma.

Duras, M. and Gauthier, X. (1974), *Les Parleuses*, Paris, Minuit.

Duras, M. and Noguez, D. (1984a), *La Couleur des mots*, interview filmed by Beaujour, J. and Mascolo, J., Le Bureau d'animation culturelle du ministère des relations extérieures.

Duras, M. and Noguez, D. (1984b), *Le Cimetière anglais*, Beaujour, J. and Mascolo, J., BAC.

Duras, M. and Noguez, D. (1984c), *La Caverne noire*, Beaujour, J. and Mascolo, J., BAC.

Duras, M. and Porte, M. (1983), 'The Places of Marguerite Duras', *Enclitic*, 7(2): 55–62.

Heinrich, N. (1980), 'Aurélia Steiner', *Cahiers du cinéma*, 307 (January), 45–7.

Noguez, D. (1978), 'Les India Songs de Marguerite Duras', *Cahiers du Vingtième Siècle*, 9: 31–48.

Prédal, R. (1991), *Le Cinéma français depuis 1945*, Paris, Nathan.

Ropars-Wuilleumier, M.-C. (1979), 'La Mort des miroirs', *L'Avant scène du cinéma*, 225: 4–12.

Royer, M. (1997), *L'Ecran de la passion: une'étude du cinéma de Marguerite Duras*, Mount Nebo, Queensland, Boombana Publications.

Udris, R. (1993), *Welcome Unreason: a Study of 'Madness' in the Novels of Marguerite Duras*, Amsterdam, Rodopi.

Wiesel, E. (1958), *La Nuit*, Paris, Minuit.

1 School's out: Jeanne Moreau as the friend and Valérie Mascolo as Nathalie Granger in *Nathalie Granger* (1972)

2 A silent friendship: Lucia Bose as Isabelle Granger and Jeanne Moreau as the friend in *Nathalie Granger* (1972)

3 A stroll in the park: Didier Flamand as the young guest, Delphine Seyrig as Anne-Marie Stretter and Claude Mann as Michael Richardson in *India Song* (1975)

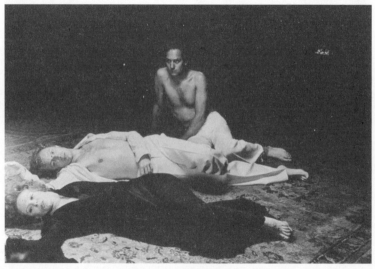

4 Two's company ... : Delphine Seyrig, Claude Mann and Didier Flamand in *India Song* (1975)

5 Despair: Michael Lonsdale as the vice-consul in *India Song* (1975)

6 Hot gossip: Marguerite Duras as the woman and Gérard Depardieu as the man in *Le Camion* (1977)

3

The politics of cinema

Working within the 1970s French avant-garde, Duras set out to dismantle the mechanisms of mainstream cinema, progressively undermining conventional representation and narrative and replacing
them with her own innovative technique. However, the experimental
impetus of her cinema was not motivated solely by artistic or aesthetic
considerations, but also had important political implications. As
Prédal has noted, because of the troubling effects of her films, critics
have tended to dismiss them as artistic provocation, 'alors que les
films de Marguerite Duras sont toujours ouvertement politiques'[1]
(Prédal 1977: 16). The political dimension of her work derived from
her understanding that film, like literature, is inseparable from the
society within which it is produced and that its representations of the
world serve not merely to entertain, but also to either reinforce or
question the ideological systems, the sets of beliefs and values that
support the structures of that society. Central to the dominant ideology in Western capitalist societies is the assumption that all art,
including cinema, is an imitation of reality, a plausible representation
of 'life'. This mimetic or reflectionist model, which can be traced back
to Aristotle, became central to the conventions of the nineteenth-
century realist novel with its view that literature should be an objective,
life-like reproduction of the world. The realist model has since been
transported from literature into mainstream cinema where it still
shapes representation, aspiring, as Susan Hayward has put it, to 'an
identification of cinema with reality' (Hayward 1993: 227). However,
as Marxist criticism has shown, realism is the privileged mode of

1 'whereas the films of Marguerite Duras are always overtly political'

representation in Western cultures and, therefore, far from mirroring an assumed universal reality, it uncritically reflects and thereby empowers bourgeois ideology.[2] Through realist art, then, society represents its own ideas and beliefs *as if* they were an immutable aspect of 'reality' or 'nature' and hence encourages readers and spectators to accept such representations as true. This means, for example, that social inequalities are not shown for what they are, but rather in terms of 'natural differences' between people which are used, in turn, to justify socially constructed hierarchies. This critical analysis may be applied to all dominant ideologies and discourses, whether capitalist, post-colonialist or patriarchal. In patriarchal cinema, for instance, violence against women is often staged as if it were prompted by a male 'instinct' for control in response to an inherently masochistic female desire to be submissive. Dominant cinema, then, obscures the fact that its representations are the product of particular social and historical circumstances and not a reflection of 'reality'. But even though the realist model has been prevalent both in the novel and in film, its cinematographic incarnation is arguably more powerful than its literary expression. Whereas the novel relies on words for its representations of the world, the primacy of the image and of the gaze in film gives us the impression that what we are shown here is a more direct and, therefore, more convincing 'window on the world'. Mainstream cinema makes use of a whole battery of technical devices which maintain this realist illusion and hence encourage the spectator to accept what is being shown as 'the truth'. Such devices achieve what Roland Barthes, in the context of the nineteenth-century novel, called 'reality effects'. In the cinema, these are all the more powerful, since they have become so much part of the viewing experience that we are hardly aware of their presence. Reality effects are created, for example, by the inclusion on a film's soundtrack of 'realistic' background noises of footsteps or banging doors. Paradoxically, our attention is drawn to the artificial nature of such noises when they are deliberately omitted from a soundtrack, as is the case in *Nathalie Granger*. Other familiar devices include seamless editing and perfect synchronisation. These effects are heightened, moreover, by the emphasis placed in mainstream cinema on external reality, represented through action, movement and the visible unfolding of a story, at the

2 For a detailed analysis of this question, see Eagleton, 1976.

expense of the subjective inner reality that is central to the work of Duras.

As Dionys Mascolo remarked, cinema has created its own imperialism, taking over and absorbing all forms of writing into the formidable power of the image (Mascolo 1979: 144). Duras's *écriture cinématographique*, on the other hand, subverts this power by challenging representation itself. In opposition to the devices commonly used in mainstream film, Duras deploys a series of deliberately anti-realist techniques, replacing the familiar reality effects with her own rather unsettling 'alienation effects', reminiscent of the theatre of Bertolt Brecht.[3] The most prominent of these, as we have seen, is her use of the *voix off* which disrupts the continuity between body and voice normally obtained by synchronisation. Similarly, the deliberate, highly stylised movements and gestures performed by the actors in *Nathalie Granger*, for example, 'denaturalise' the film since they prevent us from identifying with the protagonists as if they were real people. In their most radical form, Duras's alienation effects undermine the very foundations of cinema as the art of the image. In *Le Camion*, for instance, instead of pretending to show us a slice of reality, Duras films herself in the process of telling a story. Finally, if commercial cinema is primarily a capitalist enterprise, ruled by 'la loi de l'argent', the 'law of money' (Mascolo 1979: 144), the well-known Durassian method of recycling images and soundtracks may be interpreted not only in terms of the intratextual structure of her work, but also as a gesture of opposition to the enormous financial investment in mainstream film productions which she described as 'le maquereautage phénoménal du cinéma par le capitalisme'[4] (Lebelley 1994: 236).

While all films by Duras can be described as 'political' or 'oppositional', in the sense that they subvert dominant modes of representation, *Nathalie Granger*, *Le Camion* and *Les Mains négatives* differ from the rest of her work, as they combine this formal challenge with

---

3 As a Communist playwright, Brecht wanted to destroy the realist and naturalist illusion created by German bourgeois theatre in the 1930s through his own 'epic theatre'. His works included a series of typical 'alienation effects', for instance song and dance, that would interrupt the play's action, thereby distancing the audience from it and encouraging them to reflect critically on what was being presented on stage instead of accepting it as an unproblematic representation of reality.

4 'the phenomenal prostitution of the cinema by capitalism'

overtly political themes relating to feminism, communism and post-colonialism. In spite of this shared thematic focus, however, we can trace a certain transformation in the politics of Durassian cinema throughout the 1970s. *Nathalie Granger* is clearly an example of early feminist film, produced in opposition to patriarchal cinema and its constructions of women. Although the film attempts to break down patriarchal gender categories, because of its oppositional and separatist stance, *Nathalie Granger* remains to some extent caught up within the very ideology it sets out to question. With *Le Camion*, on the other hand, Duras begins to dismantle an entire political framework, based on dualistic thinking, by showing how any reversal of power relationships only reinforces the existence of social hierarchies. Thus, in *Le Camion*, oppressed groups become oppressors, in turn, as the bourgeoisie is replaced by the 'dictatorship of the proletariat'. Her cinema, as Matthieu Orléan has suggested, represents a critique of a notion of politics that reduces the world to a series of irreconcilable opposites: 'Le monde est divisé, fou, et la politique est une science inhumaine qui a pour objet cette folie incalculable'[5] (Orléan 1998: 4). The fact that in her films Duras denounces this 'mad divided world' does not imply, however, that she denies difference or rejects 'otherness'. Although she objected to the rigid categorisation of individuals into social groups and the tacit assumption that all members of such groups are identical (Perrot 1988), she recognised the complex and contradictory nature of identities, both individual and collective. She suggests, therefore, that the hierarchical model of politics, with its inbuilt striving for power, should be replaced by a different mode of interaction, based on an understanding not only of diversity among people, but also of their interdependence. Like her politics, her cinema is plural, multidimensional and ambiguous, in contrast with the 'either–or' framework of thought that has shaped Western cultures.

Nathalie Granger

The making of *Nathalie Granger* in 1972 coincided with the period of intense political activity and lively theoretical debates which marked the early years of the post–1968 French feminist movement. In the

5 'The world is divided, mad, and politics is an inhuman science whose object is this incalculable madness.'

previous year the campaign for the legalisation of abortion had come to a head when the magazine *Le Nouvel observateur* published a petition signed by 343 women, including Marguerite Duras, all of whom declared that they had had an abortion, thereby risking prosecution, and possibly a prison sentence, under the draconian French abortion act of 1920. In 1972, five thousand women from all over France joined a two-day meeting and mass demonstrations in Paris to protest against violence towards women and, in particular, against the way in which rape was being trivialised within the French judicial system. But although the French Women's Movement, the Mouvement de libération des femmes (MLF), was an inspiration to filmmakers like Duras and Varda, the relationship between their work and their feminist politics was quite different from that of their British or American counterparts. Whereas the latter wanted to film women's issues, often in the form of documentaries, women directors in France, as Jill Forbes has pointed out, were concerned rather with the cinematic discourse itself, since one of their primary objectives was to transform the visual constructions of gender in dominant cinema (Forbes 1992: 77). This is certainly true of *Nathalie Granger* which reflects the experimental and innovative quality of Duras's film language rather than the realist styles of Anglo-American feminist cinema of the early 1970s.

Despite the united front presented by the MLF in their political activism, particularly around single-issue campaigns such as abortion, the French feminist movement was divided, from its inception in the late 1960s, into numerous groupings or 'currents', each with its own set of ideas and theories. Among these, two opposing camps have left their imprint on the recent history of French feminism, even after the virtual demise of the MLF in the early 1980s. The first of these is the radical feminist current which, inspired by Simone de Beauvoir in *Le Deuxième sexe*, holds the view that all definitions of gender, the categories of 'masculine' and 'feminine', have been manufactured by patriarchal societies in order to perpetuate their own existence, since it is usually the perception that women are naturally different from men that is invoked to justify the oppression of women. For radical feminists, therefore, women's liberation depends upon the abolition of gender categories and the subsequent creation of a gender-neutral world, where ultimately even the concepts of 'man' and 'woman' would become irrelevant to our existence as human beings.[6] At the opposite end of the spectrum, 'differentialist' feminists argue that the most important task for women today is to reclaim their difference, not by accepting patriarchal constructs of 'femininity' as an inferior version of 'masculinity', but by creating their own specific identities in harmony with their experiences as women. Luce Irigaray, in particular, defends the idea that men and women should develop different subjectivities, since otherwise women would simply continue to be subsumed under the category of 'man', as has been the case throughout the history of patriarchy.

When we look at Duras's cinema from a feminist perspective, however, it is impossible to read her films unequivocally through either of these two theories. As with her life and work in general, her particular brand of feminism is idiosyncratic and bears her characteristic stamp of ambiguity. Thus, on the one hand, she did share the view that women's experience is fundamentally different from that of men, which may be due to both biological and social influences. The specific modes of being she associated with women, such as 'silence' and 'passivity', were seen both as stemming from the history of women's oppression and as representing strategies of resistance. However, for Duras, 'passivity' does not in any way signify the idea of a 'natural' feminine submissiveness, but rather a form of passive resistance which would consist in women's refusal to cooperate with the demands placed upon them by the patriarchal order. As she commented in Les Parleuses, 'l'inertie, les refus, le refus passif, le refus de répondre en somme, est une force colossale, c'est la force de l'enfant par exemple, c'est la force de la femme'[7] (Duras and Gauthier 1974: 109–10). But while this perception of women as a gender-specific group with their own experiences and modes of expression is compatible with the ideology of 'difference', Duras's resistance to all concepts of identity leads her to question fixed definitions of gender. This ambiguity, which is at the heart of Nathalie Granger, has informed the two complementary readings of the film that are proposed in this book. On the one hand, as I will argue in the present chapter, the film is clearly an example of what Elizabeth Kaplan has termed 'women's counter-cinema' (Kaplan 1983: 33); that is, the various practices adopted by women directors to subvert patriarchal constructions

6 For a detailed analysis of this position, see Wittig, 1992.
7 'inertia, refusal, passive refusal, all in all the refusal to respond is a colossal force, it's the force of the child, for example, it's the force of the woman'

of women in mainstream film and to create female-centred forms of representation. Nevertheless, *Nathalie Granger* is also an early attempt in Duras's cinema to transcend the boundaries of gender by implicitly deconstructing the spectator's perceptions of 'masculinity' and 'femininity'. Therefore, although the film represents an important contribution to the politics of Durassian cinema, it also reaches beyond the constraints of political ideologies towards the sense of openness that permeates her later work.

If *Nathalie Granger* was released during an important moment in the recent history of the French women's movement, the film's location is equally significant from a feminist perspective. It was shot in Duras's house and garden at the village of Neauphle, near Paris. For Duras, as she commented in *La Classe de la violence*, the house became a symbol for all the women who lived and died there over the centuries and who, because they were unable to write, disappeared without trace. It was partly to underline the historical continuity that links these silent female generations to contemporary women, like the filmic character of Isabelle Granger (Lucia Bose), that Duras made *Nathalie Granger*, 'parce qu'il y a une continuité des femmes qui sont passées par là, qui sont mortes là, qui ne disaient rien, qui ont vécu là dans une sorte d'équivalence, finalement, à ce que nous vivons, nous'[8] (Duras and Noguez 1984). Despite the undeniable progress made by women since the late twentieth century, *Nathalie Granger* presents us with a world that still conforms to the traditional social divisions between men and women. These divisions are introduced near the beginning of the film during a sequence shot inside the dining room of the Granger's house. Following a brief exchange between Mr Granger (Dionys Mascolo) and Isabelle's nameless friend (Jeanne Moreau) about Nathalie's (Valérie Mascolo) impending expulsion from school, we see the father leave the house and get in his car, presumably to go to work. Immediately after his departure, the gaze of the camera moves from the street back into the house, resting on a long 'take' of the two women looking out of the dining-room window. At this early stage in the film, the constellation of images presented has already constructed a pattern of oppositions between the house and the street, the 'inside' and the 'outside', the private domestic world

8 'because there is a continuity between the women who passed through there, who died there, who said nothing, whose lives were quite similar to ours, after all'

inhabited by women and children and the public domain associated with men. The text of *Nathalie Granger*, published after the film's release, notes that in the father's absence, the house is transformed into 'la maison des femmes', 'the women's house' (Duras 1973: 18). But the significance of the house in relation to the personal and collective history of women is more ambiguous than it appears at first sight. On the one hand, the house might well be seen to signify a female space, an environment which, because of its perennial association with women, has shaped their specific experiences and modes of being. There are moments in *Nathalie Granger* when the quiet still-ness of the house is reflected in the women's calm, slow movements and their non-verbal communication expressed through their looks, smiles and gestures. The house also becomes the place where the increasing sense of solidarity between the women finally erupts in Isabelle Granger's gesture of revolt against the outside world. This view of the house as an image linking women's space and female identity is endorsed by Duras herself who, in '*Les Lieux de Marguerite Duras*, posits a certain fusional relationship between Isabelle Granger and her home, 'comme si la maison elle-même avait forme de femme'[9] (Duras and Porte 1977: 20). Yet, for the most part, the house appears like a prison, reinforcing Isabelle's growing sense of isolation and alienation. The oppressiveness associated with the house is conveyed quite powerfully through the recurring shots of window frames which resemble the barred windows in a prison cell and which partially block Isabelle's view of the street outside. In fact, during the first part of the film, Isabelle is filmed solely inside the house, her heavy, ponderous movements expressing her increasing mental and physical paralysis: 'Isabelle Granger passe. Elle est donc sortie de la cuisine, de l'immobilité. Elle traverse, disparaît [...] Déambulation de prisonnière. Elle repart, regarde cette maison, cette caverne, la sienne'[10] (Duras 1973: 27). This sense of entrapment is expressed through the tracking shots down empty corridors and passages that lead to closed doors, implying the absence of any viable escape route for Isabelle. Like the hotel in Duras's text and film *Détruire dit-elle*, the Granger house is a cold, lonely and somewhat sinister place, which militates

9 'as if the house itself had a woman's shape'
10 'Isabelle Granger walks past. She has come out of the kitchen, out of the immobility [...] A prisoner's stroll. She sets off again, looks at this house, this cave, hers.'

against the patriarchal construct of the home as women's natural environment, associated with feminine warmth and nurturing. In this respect, the contrast in *Nathalie Granger* between the feminine domestic world and the masculine public sphere corresponds to the distinction made by Simone de Beauvoir in *Le Deuxième sexe* between the states of immanence and transcendence (Beauvoir 1976: 31). Within Beauvoir's theoretical framework, immanence defines the physical and psychological confinement of women in patriarchal societies, whereas transcendence indicates the freedom, traditionally the prerogative of men, to fulfil one's potential through creative expression. Considering the largely negative significance of the house in *Nathalie Granger*, the film's ending is rather ambiguous. While it is true, as Elizabeth Kaplan has argued, that when Isabelle tears up the newspaper, the electricity bill and her daughter's school exercise book, she cuts all ties with the dominant male order (Kaplan 1983: 102), the women's detachment from society leaves them potentially incapable of discovering the state of transcendence which, for Beauvoir, was an essential prerequisite of women's liberation. Instead, Isabelle's separatist gesture would conceivably deepen the feeling of alienation from which she is attempting to escape. That the women's complete isolation from the outside world is to be viewed with some reservation is suggested in the final sequence of the film when both the salesman (Gérard Depardieu) and the passing dog appear frightened by the women's house (Duras 1973: 88). But although Duras seems to imply here that communication between 'inside' and 'outside' is both necessary and desirable, ultimately the film's construction of space upholds the distinction between specifically male and female domains.

Similar divisions in relation to gender operate in Duras's filming of time in *Nathalie Granger*. Like many women writers and directors, she has created representations of time which break with the patriarchal notion of the temporal order as a linear, chronological structure divisible into past, present and future. Instead, she merges these different compartments of time into the duration of an apparently eternal present. As Irma Garcia has argued, women's rejection of linear time might be due to the narrow continuity imposed on the social patterning of their lives, as the short-lived freedom of childhood is soon replaced by the endless monotony of their domestic situation (Garcia 1981: 204–5). Similarly, Claudine Herrmann has pointed out that, while the prevalent gender model has allowed men to experience life as process and discovery, it has condemned many women to a repetitive and relatively static existence (Herrmann 1976: 161). This emptiness of 'women's time' is powerfully evoked in *Nathalie Granger* which shows a typical afternoon in the life of Isabelle Granger and, by extension, that of other women. After lunch, following the departure of Isabelle's husband and children, the women are left on their own with only a few household tasks to occupy their time. Ahead of them lies a deadly void, suspended across hours of waiting for the family's return: 'Du temps passe, temps pendant lequel la vaisselle se termine et que s'ouvre cette béance: l'après-midi d'hiver'[11] (Duras 1973: 26). As Duras has suggested elsewhere, the boredom and repetitiveness of women's domestic situation is reminiscent of that endured by prisoners, an experience which may well lead to the development of suicidal tendencies (Duras and Gauthier 1974: 98–9). *Nathalie Granger* does, in fact, hint at the corrosive effect of time on Isabelle's mental state, as her face increasingly reflects her loneliness and entrapment while the script notes that she may be heading towards a nervous breakdown (Duras 1973: 36).

Duras's construction of time in *Nathalie Granger* both highlights and implicitly criticises the restrictive temporal order imposed on women, particularly in relation to the pattern of constant repetition inherent in housework. One of Duras's objectives in making this film was, in fact, to show this fundamental aspect of women's lives, which is usually ignored or marginalised in both mainstream cinema and society. It was a startling innovation in the early 1970s to see one of the great icons of French cinema, Jeanne Moreau, clearing a table, washing up and putting away the dishes. What Duras shows here is the other side of patriarchal femininity, what she called 'une féminité fonctionnelle [...] au service de l'homme'[12] (Duras and Gauthier 1974: 73). To this she devotes an entire two-minute sequence, filmed in real time, during which the camera lingers painstakingly on the women's hands, clearing the table with slow deliberate movements. The sequence is further decomposed into close-up shots of each individual gesture, as the women pick up the crockery and glasses, take them to the kitchen, return to the table, wipe the crumbs off the

11 'Time goes by, time during which the washing-up is finished and this gaping void opens up: the winter afternoon.'
12 'a functional femininity, at the service of men'

surface and place them in a small dish. Although Duras clearly does not suggest that women's activities should be limited to housework, she nevertheless gives it the recognition which is generally lacking in societies that consider 'women's work' irrelevant and unproductive. The long 'take' of the empty table bears witness to the way in which housework is usually considered non-existent in the absence of any tangible 'product'. The table's primary function during this shot as a metaphor of women's invisibility rather than as a 'real' object foregrounds the anti-realist quality of *Nathalie Granger*. Duras was not interested in making a feminist documentary about housework, but rather in showing the mental and emotional effects of this aspect of women's experience. The images, therefore, function as signifiers of that experience rather than as representations of external reality. To enhance this anti-realism even further, Duras omitted from the sound-track noises that we take for granted and that normally contribute to the reality effects within a film, for instance the sound of footsteps in the corridors or the clattering of the dishes in the sink, as Jeanne Moreau is busy with the washing-up.

The social organisation of women's time is reflected not only in the contents of *Nathalie Granger*, but also in its cinematic discourse. If the chronological narrative structures of mainstream film can be related to the linear temporal framework of patriarchal societies, the patterns of circularity and repetition characteristic of Durassian cinema clearly correspond to women's experience of time. The story of *Nathalie Granger* is told not through coherently linked visual sequences, but rather through the constellation and juxtaposition of particular images and sounds which are charged with symbolic significance and whose repetition at important points creates the film's meanings. Thus, for example, the images of the pylons, the radio and the pram as well as the obsessive repetition of the music are implicitly linked to the theme of violence early in the film, recurring at regular intervals to signal characters or events associated with violence. As Kaplan has remarked, *Nathalie Granger* is structured more like a poem than a realist narrative (Kaplan 1983: 95), thus defying the patterns of causal logic which underpin a whole tradition of representation in Western cultures. Although Duras criticises the restrictive temporal order imposed on women, her film does not suggest that she simply advocates replacing its circularity and duration with the linear, future-orientated model prevalent in the 'masculine' world of work and achievement.

But since *Nathalie Granger* does not offer any synthesis of these two temporal orders, we can only assume that, unlike Beauvoir, Duras did not see transcendence as a viable alternative to the state of immanence of which her film is nevertheless an indictment.

In *Nathalie Granger*, then, constructions of time and space are somewhat ambiguous, since they could be viewed as simultaneously questioning and reinforcing the binary divisions underlying the patriarchal social order. Duras's filming of the female body, on the other hand, represents an unequivocal example of women's counter-cinema. As feminist film theory, beginning with the work of Laura Mulvey, has repeatedly demonstrated, 'women are inevitably reduced to the objects of a male gaze in mainstream cinema' (Humm 1997: 39). Durassian cinema, however, as exemplified in *Nathalie Granger*, clearly shows that it is possible to film women differently. For instead of representing the two actresses in her film as the objects of an eroticised spectacle, she films their bodies as the physical manifestations of the experiences, perceptions and situations that are likely to characterise women's everyday lives. The female body in *Nathalie Granger*, instead of being subjected to voyeuristic scrutiny, is represented in such a way that we see it as an integral part of female subjectivity. As Royer has pointed out, Durassian cinema on the whole shows a preference for medium and distant shots over close-ups, thereby liberating the spectator from the compulsive gaze built into mainstream 'scopophilic' cinema (Royer 1997: 75). While this is certainly the case in many of Duras's films, *Nathalie Granger* presents the viewer with an unusual array of close-up shots, especially of her female protagonists' hands and faces. The purpose and effect of these shots, however, is to question the conventional function of close-up filming of women, frequently employed both in dominant cinema and in advertising. This technique visually dissects the female body so as to draw the attention of the gaze to its eroticised parts, for example breasts or legs, which then come to represent the whole body and, by extension, the woman herself. Duras's use of close-up shots, on the contrary, subverts this fetishistic and dehumanising film practice, commonly used by directors like Truffaut and Blier, by deploying it as a strategy of feminist counter-cinema. For example, the recurring images of female hands in *Nathalie Granger*, instead of operating as signifiers of the objectified female body, underline instead the film's dialectical movement from oppression to resistance. Close-up shots of hands are used here to highlight the limited sphere of women's domestic activities, such as clearing the table and, later in the film, ironing and sewing. That we frequently see the hands separate from the rest of the body, and thus from the individual identities of the women shown, suggests the depersonalising nature of housework, emphasising all the more clearly that these activities are shared by most, if not all, women. Hence, far from reproducing the fetishism usually associated with the close-up, Duras politicises it, using it to create a potential feeling of solidarity among women, including her female spectators. The significance of the hands as signifiers of both oppression and revolt becomes apparent at several points in the film. First, when the two women are clearing the table, the images of their hands alternate with shots of a black cat which, in the film script, is repeatedly associated with the violence that is also expressed by Nathalie and later by Isabelle: 'La Violence habite les yeux du chat'[13] (Duras 1973: 22). In the latter half of the film, during the sequence showing the two sisters, Nathalie and Laurence, during their piano lesson, the close-up of the teacher's hands, forcing Nathalie to play her piece, signify the oppressiveness of the adult, middle-class society against which Nathalie rebels. After the teacher's departure, the girl suddenly plays her seven notes, as her hands, previously 'imprisoned' (Duras 1973: 72), now express the violence of her revolt. But the most startling use of the close-up occurs when Isabelle Granger joins her daughter's resistance by tearing up and burning the symbols of a society from which she is, in any case, excluded, both as a woman and as a foreigner. Her strong, determined gestures clearly contrast with her visible paralysis earlier in the film, indicating the intensity of her repressed anger. Also in contrast with previous close-up sequences are the rapid shots and jump cuts which suddenly accelerate the rhythm of the image-track, introducing an abrupt sense of release after the sustained tension of this otherwise deliberately slow-moving film. But it is not only the female hands which announce the eruption of violence after what Duras described as 'une oppression immémoriale', 'an age-old oppression' (Duras 1973: 90). The recurring close-up shots of the faces of Nathalie, Isabelle and her friend also signify their emotional states, in particular the contained anger perceptible in their looks and its potential expression as revolt against the social constructs of femininity. In *Nathalie Granger* it is the very immobility

13 'Violence inhabits the cat's eyes.'

to which patriarchy has condemned women's bodies that threatens to erupt into what Duras would consider a liberating and hence necessary counter-violence, albeit in the form of passive resistance. Apart from these close-up images with their implicitly political significance, the film does not contain any shots, fetishistic or otherwise, which represent only parts of the female body. The women in *Nathalie Granger* are typically filmed through medium or long-distance shots and the outlines of their bodies are often blurred or reflected in a mirror. The mirror as a framing device is used here, as in other films by Duras, to demonstrate that all forms of representation, including film, are themselves reflections of other, previous representations and not, as the conventions of mainstream cinema would have us believe, transparent reproductions of 'reality'. Applied to a feminist reading of *Nathalie Granger*, then, Duras's use of the mirror as a distancing device draws our attention to the fact that what we see here are simply a particular director's constructions of women and of the female body and not images of 'real' women.

With *Nathalie Granger*, Duras attacked the twin pillars of mainstream cinematic representations of women. Not only did she refuse to film women as objects of the gaze, but she also enabled her female protagonists to become subjects of their own gaze. Her film thus demonstrates that the gaze is not tied exclusively to the masculine subject position, but that it is an integral part of feminine subjectivity as well. However, as we shall see, Duras's filming of the female gaze in *Nathalie Granger* is rather different from the controlling, appropriatory act of looking that feminist theorists have rightly associated with patriarchal film discourses (Hayward 1993: 228). For if dominant representations rely upon a clear distinction between the active subject of the gaze and its passive object, there are several visual sequences in *Nathalie Granger* which suggest that Duras is, in fact, dismantling the division between subject and object itself. This process can be illustrated by reference to a number of key moments in the film, structured around the female gaze. The first such scene occurs immediately after the 'table clearing' sequence, as Isabelle Granger's ghost-like figure wanders aimlessly round the house and eventually stops in the kitchen. The camera eye now oscillates between the objects in the kitchen and Isabelle's face and eventually coincides with the woman's gaze slowly gliding across the objects. The point of view constructed in this sequence, then, alternates between that adopted by the camera and that of Isabelle, as both are placed in the position of the active viewing subject. But the construction of Isabelle at this point is complicated by the fact that she is simultaneously the subject and the object of the gaze. The spectator looks both at her, that is at the close-up shot of her face, and with her, as she casts her gaze around the kitchen. This ambiguous construction recurs at various points in the film, particularly in the numerous sequences where the gaze is doubled by the camera, a mirror or another gaze. Thus, as Isabelle's friend stares out of the window, we see her reflection in a mirror, while Isabelle looks at her looking. Duras's technique here clearly disrupts the fixed division between a voyeuristic camera and the objectified woman characteristic of patriarchal cinema.

The female gaze in *Nathalie Granger* is not only an essential aspect of women's subjectivity, but it also has the power to act upon and transmute inanimate objects. As the script indicates, the alarm clock in the kitchen only begins to tick when Isabelle looks at it (Duras 1973: 26) and even the things in Nathalie's room come alive under Isabelle's gaze. Other objects associated with the two women, such as the table, the radio and even the house itself seem to take on a life of their own and are thus transformed from mere things into filmic 'subjects' in their own right. Indeed, the house at Neauphle, as Noguez has noted, might even be described as 'le lieu central, le personnage principal du film'[14] (Duras and Noguez 1984). Ultimately, the film deconstructs not only gender-specific divisions, but also the distinction between people and things. If the camera in *Nathalie Granger* creates images of women as subjects of the gaze, the latter, in turn, endows even objects with a sense of agency. From a semantic point of view, the objects in *Nathalie Granger* play an essential role, in so far as they become signifiers of the protagonists and their experiences. They partly replace the film narrative, as they 'tell the story' by generating the visual patterns that underscore its thematic structure. For example, the recurring shots of the forest beyond the Granger's house, the doll's pram and Nathalie's toys in the garden, create a complex thematic relationship linking Nathalie and the two young murderers through their shared violence.

Nathalie Granger is a powerful cinematic expression of ideas that were central to French feminism in the early 1970s. It presents us with a number of thematic and discursive strands which reflect the

14 'the central place, the main character in the film'

then popular concerns of 'difference' feminism, for instance the affirmation of specifically female domains and experiences. Although during these early years of second-wave feminism it was important for women to reclaim their identities, in the long run the ideology of difference could only serve to strengthen the gendered binarisms that underpin patriarchal societies. Translated into cinematic terms this means that while Duras's feminist countercinema was a crucial step in her attempts to film women differently, it nevertheless ran the risk of reinforcing the very divisions that her work in film tried to overcome.

Le Camion

Chosen to represent France at the Cannes Film Festival in 1977, *Le Camion* has attracted the usual admixture of praise and scathing criticism which surrounds Durassian cinema. At Cannes the film was denounced for representing too extreme an example of 'literary cinema' and, as Prédal has pointed out, its reception was an ironic rerun of the fate of Resnais's *Hiroshima mon amour* which was booed at the 1959 Festival, while *Orpheo Negro* by Marcel Camus was awarded the prestigious *Palme d'Or* (Prédal 1977: 16). But it was not only at Cannes that *Le Camion* provoked adverse reactions. At the 1977 New York Film Festival, 'the audience reacted with exasperation and irritation, bursting into embarrassed laughter or walking out of the theater' (Finel-Honigman 1979: 131). It is true that, even to audiences used to Duras's iconoclasm, *Le Camion* looks more provocative than her previous work. If *Nathalie Granger*, for instance, can be described as countercinema, *Le Camion* is virtual cinema, the end of representation as we know it. For, instead of a 'film', we see images of Duras herself and of Gérard Depardieu, reading a draft of the script which tells the story of an elderly woman hitching a lift with a young lorry driver who is also a member of the Communist Party. During their brief journey together she talks to him about politics, the likely failure of all revolutions and a child called Abraham. These reading sequences, filmed in Duras's converted loft at Neauphle, are intercut with tracking shots of a blue lorry travelling through the desolate industrial landscape in the Yvelines region between Trappes and Plaisir, accompanied by Beethoven's Variations on a Diabelli Waltz. The hypothetical nature of the film is introduced early on, when during the reading sequence in the 'chambre noire', 'the dark room'(Duras 1977: 11), Depardieu and Duras engage in the following dialgoue:

> GD: C'est un film?
> MD: C'aurait été un film.
> [...]
> C'est un film, oui.[15]
>
> (Duras 1977: 11–12)

Throughout the text of *Le Camion*, as this extract indicates, Duras uses the conditional perfect and the present tense interchangeably, thus underlining a fundamental equivalence in the film between actual reality and the virtual reality of the imagination. This, as she pointed out to Michelle Porte, is similar to the way in which children at play accept their own imagination as real (Duras 1977: 89). The conditional tense in the film thus blurs the borderline between fiction and reality, suggesting that all cinema is an imaginary construct and that, therefore, *Le Camion* is no more 'unreal' than a Hollywood movie or a film by Truffaut. The open, hypothetical quality of the text would have been destroyed by conventional representation. Reading and listening to the text produces a potentially unlimited number of images, of the woman hitchhiker, for instance, which would have been reduced to one image had Duras made a representational film. As she said in an interview with Prédal: 'Dans *Le Camion* [...] je mets l'imaginaire à son comble, je lui donne le maximum de chances'[16] (Prédal 1977: 18). The film's virtuality, then, opens up the spectator's creativity both in relation to the image and to different ways of reading the story which could be interpreted as a political allegory or, indeed, as a love story between the lorry driver and the woman. Although Duras had already questioned the image/sound hierarchy in previous films, *Le Camion* is the first work where she completely reverses it, transforming cinema into an auditory, not a visual experience. The spoken word predominates throughout, as even the image of the blue lorry has no independent significance, operating as a container for the text which

15 GD: 'Is this a film?
    MD: 'It would have been a film.'
    'Yes, it's a film.'
16 'In *Le Camion* I foreground the imagination above all else, I give it every oppor-tunity.'

it carries from the darkened room to the exterior tracking shots of the winter landscape (Duras 1977: 101). But this paradoxical film about an absent film was made not just because Duras wanted to go beyond the limits of conventional cinema, since the freedom from representation attained in *Le Camion* has political as well as artistic implications. For Duras, political ideologies mirror cinematic representation, in so far as both fabricate particular versions of reality, telling people who they are and how to see the world. Her rejection of representation in *Le Camion*, therefore, reflects her general critique of political systems and their underlying power structures.

This denunciation of political power in *Le Camion* begins with Duras's vehement criticism of the PCF which can be traced back to her resignation and subsequent expulsion from the party in 1950, after her seven-year experience as a fervent activist. The sense of loss she experienced following this episode was exacerbated by the fact that for her the PCF had become a substitute family, creating a strong personal identification in addition to her political commitment (Duras 1977: 117). Nearly thirty years after leaving the party, therefore, Duras still felt guilty at the thought of being denounced as a political traitor. As she explained to Michelle Porte, the making of *Le Camion* was a form of catharsis, as if the fear that she might be accused of anti-Communism had finally been laid to rest: 'Je n'ai plus peur. Je n'ai plus peur qu'on me taxe d'anticommunisme. Le fameux axiome stalinien: "Si tu n'es pas pour nous, tu es avec eux", c'est fini, il me fait rire dorénavant'[17] (Duras 1977: 112). The woman in *Le Camion*, who might be Duras's 'alter ego' (Lebelley 1994: 265), is no longer afraid to show her irreverence for the sacred relics of communist ideology, as she criticises the 'dictatorship of the proletariat', the revolutionary ideal and the militant party activist who, in her imaginary film, would have been represented by the sullen, taciturn lorry driver invented in the script. Reminiscent of some of the Communist characters in Sartre's fiction, for example Brunet in *L'Age de raison*, Duras's lorry driver lives in a state of alienation, since he has given up his freedom and individuality in exchange for the reassuring sense of belonging to a party which provides him with a clearly defined identity. Blinded by party dogma he is disconnected from the world and others around

17 'I'm no longer afraid. I'm no longer afraid of being accused of anti-Communism. The famous Stalinist axiom: "If you're not for us, you're with them" is finished; it now makes me laugh.'

him, as demonstrated by the fact that he can see only what he is ordered to see (Duras 1977: 56). But the lorry driver is only one example of the wider alienation experienced by the politicised working class whose knowledge about their oppression, according to Duras, stems from a simplified version of Marxist theory. Like the driver whose lorry transports 'des colis tout faits', 'ready-made packages' (Duras 1977: 37), the Communist Party carries with it a host of ready-made ideas and identities which reduce the diversity of individuals to their membership of a particular social group. It is not surprising, then, that the woman hitchhiker's refusal to fit any preconceived definitions is seen as a threat by the lorry driver who obsessively questions her about her identity: 'Il dit: j'ai besoin de savoir, j'ai le droit de savoir. Je suis même en droit de vous demander vos papiers d'identité'[18] (Duras 1977: 61). Her resistance to his authoritarian demands, allied with her 'blasphemous' criticism of Karl Marx, prompt the lorry driver to try and contain her by labelling her a 'reactionary', a 'madwoman' who has escaped from the local psychiatric hospital (Duras 1977: 48). The woman's alleged mental illness is interesting here in two respects. First, it suggests an allusion to and an implicit condemnation of the notorious Soviet practice of incarcerating political dissidents in psychiatric institutions. And, second, as Duras has remarked, in patriarchal cultures women themselves are often perceived as dangerous and hence declared 'insane' (Prédal 1977: 21). What is described in Le Camion as the woman's 'mental confusion' is simply her transgression of the rules of rationality and logic underlying the dominant frameworks of thought (Duras 1977: 53). Her 'illness', therefore, consists in her inability or unwillingness to impose artificial structures on the fleeting appearance of thoughts and words in the mind. Instead, her thought and speech reflect the pattern of metonymic association which has been identified by Luce Irigaray as a feature of women's writing (Jones 1985: 87). Indeed, the entire text of Le Camion itself mirrors this metonymic web, working against the logical structures of conventional narrative. Because of her refusal to conform, nobody listens to the woman whose words are described as 'banal' and 'too personal' by those who uphold the illusion of objectivity that characterises Western patriarchal thought.

18 'He says: I need to know, I have the right to know. I'm even entitled to ask you for your identity papers.'

However, Duras's critique in *Le Camion* is not limited to the dogmatism of the PCF, but extends to all political parties and ideologies, as the woman in the film-script repeatedly comments on what she sees as the collusion between communism and capitalism. For Duras, political systems are based on the same fear of the contradictions, complexities and differences that exist in society as well as within each individual. She maintains, therefore, that all ideologies, whether on the left or on the right, attempt to simplify this diversity by reducing it to their rigid theoretical frameworks. In *Le Camion* the underlying aim which unites the dominant and the oppressed class is described in the following terms: 'En chaque homme assassiner l'autre homme, le mutiler de sa donnée fondamentale: sa propre contradiction'[19] (Duras 1977: 44). Communism and capitalism are linked by a common desire for power, as each system excludes those who are perceived as somehow 'different' from the arbitrary norms of identity they construct. Thus, the woman in *Le Camion* tells the lorry driver that her son-in-law, also a member of the PCF, was reluctant to name his child Abraham, for fear of the party's predictable disapproval, motivated by its own unacknowledged anti-Semitism (Duras 1977: 54). This reference in the text to Jewish names and identities in relation to the PCF is followed by images of trains and obvious allusions to the Holocaust, underlining what Duras perceived as the similarities between Stalinist communism and Fascism, in so far as both project their fears of 'difference' through racism and anti-Semitism (Duras 1977: 56–8). The dangers of such projection can only be avoided if everyone recognises his or her own internal contradictions, 'the other' within oneself. The theme of racist oppression and exclusion in *Le Camion* is also reflected in the film's location, since the lorry's journey takes us through a region inhabited entirely by immigrants, including a large Portuguese community. As Duras explained, the latter used to live in caravans near the railway station at Plaisir, but were evicted and rehoused in the *grands ensembles*, the blocks of flats which we occasionally see in the film (Duras and Noguez, 1984a). Exiled from their native country and subsequently excluded from mainstream French society, the immigrants are condemned to live in this desolate landscape, evoked in the text by the woman's repeated vision of 'la fin du monde', 'the end of the world'

19 'To assassinate the other person within each of us, to mutilate our most fundamental element: our own contradiction.'

(Duras 1977: 20). As the camera travels along the concrete desert, it focuses on two occasions on the Auchan hypermarket, where they spend their wages on everything from furniture to coffins (Duras 1977: 109). The megastore becomes a symbol of the way in which the immigrant working class in France, abandoned by the PCF, has been absorbed by a capitalist society that encourages it to participate in its consumer culture.

Duras's disillusionment with politics is expressed in the somewhat peremptory statement: 'Que le monde aille à sa perte, c'est la seule politique'[20] (Duras 1977: 25, 67). This recurring phrase does not imply, however, that Duras is presenting us with an apocalyptic vision of the world's final destruction. What she wants to destroy, on the contrary, is the entire array of political ideologies, 'cet espèce de ramassis, de poubelles géantes de toute l'idéologie du vingtième siècle',[21] which obscure the real divisions and inequalities that exist throughout the world (Duras et al. 1979: 114). Le Camion, therefore, was intended to be what Duras called 'un acte contre tout pouvoir', a creative act against all power, both in the arena of politics and of cinema. In spite of her opposition to the PCF and, indeed, all existing political formations, Duras nevertheless retained her lifelong belief in communist ethics. But, contrary to the closed ideological systems that she attacks in Le Camion for reducing diverse realities to one absolutist theory, she upheld an ideal communism which would combine equality with respect for differences. This concept of 'equality', however, would extend beyond the material sphere of opportunities and wealth to encompass 'une égalité relative', 'a relative equality' based on an appreciation of the underlying similarities among all living beings, both humans and animals (Bouguereau 1990: 86). In this utopian communist world, as hypothetical as the film itself, the hierarchical divisions between groups and individuals would have been dismantled and replaced by that movement towards others which, for Duras, is the opposite of power (Duras 1977: 120). In this respect, it is the woman in Le Camion, described as 'déclassée' (Duras 1977: 31), who is the true revolutionary and not the lorry driver. By using the term 'déclassé' here in the sense of 'classless', Duras implicitly upholds the revolutionary Marxist ideal of a classless society, while attacking

20 'Let the world go to its ruin, that's the only form of politics.'
21 'this kind of jumble, these giant rubbish bins containing all the ideologies of the twentieth century'

its betrayal by Stalinist communism. Indeed, *Le Camion* itself is
described as 'déclassé', suggesting that both the film and its female
protagonist, defy any attempts to define and classify them according
to existing categories (Duras 1977: 129). As Michelle Porte has observed, the film addresses everybody, contrary to the critical view
expressed at Cannes and elsewhere, that it is an example of 'literary'
or 'intellectual' cinema: 'La manière dont le film est fait rejoint la
narration populaire, la tradition des conteurs, tout le monde peut
entrer là-dedans, tout le monde est concerné'[22] (Duras 1977: 130).
That the woman in the film is not an 'intellectual'is also implicit in the
fact that, although she talks continuously about a large variety of
topics, her knowledge is frequently inaccurate, suggesting that perhaps she has gleaned her information through casual conversations
rather than as a result of formal academic training (Duras 1977: 22).
In this respect, *Le Camion* echoes Duras's more general misgivings,
expressed for instance in the text *La Pluie d'été* (1990), about the one-
sided nature of academic knowledge, as it is dispensed by a middle-
class education system.

Like all of Duras's female figures, the classless woman from *Le
Camion* has no clearly definable identity. Unlike her male interlocutor
who depends on and thus clings to the political labels imposed on him
by the party, she has freed herself from the need to project a certain
persona and is, therefore, able to connect and empathise more
directly with others: 'La dame du Camion vit un amour d'ordre
général [...] Tout entière tournée vers le dehors, elle est entrée dans le
processus de disparition d'identité. Non seulement elle ne sait plus
qui elle est, mais elle cherche dans tous les sens qui elle pourrait
être'[23] (Duras *et al.* 1979: 109–10). The woman's existence, therefore,
like the film itself, is a ceaseless process of creative transformation,
not a finished product, forever fixed in its particular mould. This
absence of a specific identity corresponds to the absence of representation in the film, as Duras abandoned her original plan of having
a well-known actress, such as Simone Signoret, play the role of 'la

22 'The way in which the film is made is very much like popular narrative, the
   tradition of the storytellers, everyone can enter into it, everyone is concerned.'
23 'The lady in *Le Camion* experiences love in a general sense [...] Turned entirely
   towards the outside, she has entered the process where identity disappears. Not
   only does she no longer know who she is, but she is looking in every direction
   for who she could be.'

dame'. Like Madeleine in Duras's play *Savannah Bay* (1982), the anonymous hitch-hiker has found the freedom to let go of all false constructs of 'self' which, as Duras has remarked, comes with old age and hence the proximity of death (Duras and Noguez, 1984a). Unlike the lorry driver whose interaction with 'la dame' points to his under-lying sense of isolation, she understands that the perception of an inherent separateness between people is an illusion and that instead the world is a vast network of interlocking relationships: 'Elle dit: tout est dans tout./Partout./Tout le temps./En même temps'[24] (Duras 1977: 25–6). This key statement reflects the diversity of Duras's own background and her desire to overcome barriers and to connect with people of different classes and cultures. In *Le Camion* this closeness extends even to the relationship between the woman and the lorry driver, counteracting the latter's apparently distant attitude towards his travel companion. For regardless of a whole range of differences in terms of sex, class, age and political status, the two protagonists temporarily share the same space, the same physical environment and hence the same immediate vision: 'Ils voient le même paysage. En même temps'[25] (Duras 1977: 40). The possibility of a film, there-fore, extends to the possibility of love or, at least, of a certain com-plicity between the man and the woman. That such a bond does exist in *Le Camion* is suggested, for example, when both describe any form of revolution as 'impossible' (Duras 1977: 20) or when Duras con-firms to Depardieu that they have experienced the same alienation within the PCF (Duras 1977: 43). This similarity between the lorry driver and the woman mirrors the implicit resemblance between Duras and her fictional double which is confirmed, furthermore, by a physical description of 'la dame' in the script that is surprisingly reminiscent of Duras herself: 'Petite./Maigre./Grise./Banale./Elle a cette noblesse de la banalité./Elle est invisible'[26] (Duras 1977: 65). The description of the woman's nobility as stemming from her very ordinariness is emblematic of the figures in most of Duras's texts and films, from the maid and the travelling salesman in *Le Square* to the immigrants sweeping the streets of Paris in *Les Mains négatives*.

24 'She says: everything is in everything./Everywhere./All the time./At the same time.'
25 'They see the same countryside. At the same time.'
26 'Small./Thin./Grey./Ordinary./She has this nobility of ordinariness./She is invisible.'

Although a deeply political film, *Le Camion* advocates a different understanding of politics, one that would emphasise a sense of unity within diversity and abandon dualistic modes of perception. This underlying message is clearly mirrored in the very form and structure of the film, contrary to so-called 'political' cinema which operates as a vehicle for particular ideologies. Duras was not interested in making cinema that would represent any particular social group or 'theme', as her disillusionment with political solutions to the problems posed by human relationships coincided with her fundamental rejection of all existing forms of cinema, expressed in her famous statement: 'Que le cinéma aille à sa perte, c'est le seul cinéma'[27] (Duras *et al.* 1979: 107). Furthermore, with *Le Camion*, Duras attacks what she perceived as the mendacity of both politics and cinema, drawing a parallel between politicians who project a false identity to the public in order to sell their party's 'line' and actors playing a role that someone else has written: 'Acteurs et hommes politiques sont délégués, ils ne sont plus eux-mêmes, ils vendent leur marchandises'[28] (Duras *et al.* 1979: 113).

In *Le Camion*, on the other hand, Duras has eliminated both representation and acting. Instead of pretending to be the woman and the lorry driver, Duras and Depardieu read their dialogue in an occasionally haphazard and improvised manner. Indeed, although Duras had, of course, written the script, neither she nor Depardieu had read it before the filming of *Le Camion*. Consequently, instead of posing as the imperious, God-like figure of the film director, Duras participates with Depardieu and the spectator in the process of creation itself. This cinematic democracy is underscored by the fact that, throughout the reading sequences, the 'director' and the 'actor' seek confirmation from each other about the reality or veracity of certain details in the script (Duras 1977: 16, 19). Duras does not dictate to us how we should see her hitch-hiker, the landscape or the sea. In the absence of visual representation, the director loses the power, taken for granted in mainstream cinema, to impose on the spectator a series of fixed images or what she called 'la fixation de la représentation une fois pour toutes et pour toujours'[29] (Duras *et al.* 1979: 107). Paradoxically, then, instead of reinforcing her position as the 'author' of *Le Camion*,

27 'Let the cinema go to its ruin, that's the only cinema.'
28 'Actors and politicians are delegates, they are no longer themselves, they sell their wares.'
29 'the fixing of representation once and for all and forever'

Duras's pervasive but uncertain presence questions her control over her own film as a finished product. The fact that she reads the story of *Le Camion* in the film itself also militates against the illusion of film as a 'window on the world', showing us reality in a supposedly direct and 'objective' manner. Duras thus challenges the view of art as an imitation of life, whether in literature or in cinema, which has been upheld by capitalist as well as by communist societies, for example through the socialist realist model favoured in the former Soviet Union. The fact that bourgeois and communist ideologies overlap in their assumptions about the nature of art thus reflects the woman's remarks in *Le Camion* about the collusion between the proletariat and capitalism. Duras's appearance as a director in her own film demonstrates the necessarily subjective nature of all artistic creation, clearly evident when she talks about her ideas for the production of the film which was, of course, never made (Duras 1977: 18).

Le Camion questions the divisions around which conventional mainstream cinema operates. This subversive process, which begins with her challenge to the image/sound and the director/spectator hierarchies, is developed further as she dismantles other sets of oppositions, between inside/outside, light/darkness, subject/object, male/female. As Michelle Porte has commented, there are no clear-cut definitions in *Le Camion*, since the very boundaries of time, space and identity remain unstable throughout the film. (Duras 1977: 99). The film's visual track constantly oscillates between the interior shots of Duras and Depardieu in the darkened room and the exterior tracking sequences, just as the soundtrack alternates between Duras's voice and the music. Although Duras reads her text sitting in the room, the use of the *voix off* to accompany the lorry bridges the gap between inside and outside and hence between the two components of the visual track. A powerful illustration of Duras's technique is the tracking sequence showing the housing estate near Plaisir, as the bleak and uniform buildings are filmed against a dark-blue night sky and enveloped by Beethoven's Variations. The poetry of such images in *Le Camion* contrasts with the grim documentary style of a more overtly 'political' film, such as *La Haine* (1996) by Mathieu Kassovitz. The politics of Durassian cinema, on the other hand, consists precisely in her blending of differences, as she juxtaposes an immigrant workers' ghetto with Western classical music and thus metaphorically dissolves the barriers of class, culture and ethnicity. Her cinema, then, functions as a melting pot, since she uses sound and image to bring together a variety of cultural influences and experiences. Her creativity lies in its plurality, in the multiple forms of expression which are the hallmark of her work and which disrupt the dominant binary frameworks. This is also evident in the interior sequences where Duras and Depardieu swap places, appearing, in turn, on the right and on the left of the frame, suggesting that gendered roles and positions have also become interchangeable. Similarly, the fact that Duras's *voix off* speaks alternately from the place of the woman and that of the lorry driver (Duras 1977: 23) indicates the film's erosion of gender boundaries.

As in *Nathalie Granger*, even the distinction between people and things is abolished, as from the outset of *Le Camion* the lorry itself exudes a strangely human aura. When it first sets off from the village square during the pre-credit sequence, slowly circling a roundabout, it seems to take on a life of its own, as we see only a vague outline of someone we assume to be the driver sitting in the cab. Subsequently, the tracking sequences of the open road are seen both from within and from outside the lorry, which, therefore, becomes the subject and the object of the gaze, as the spectator looks both at it and from its point of view. Or, as Duras put it, the lorry is simultaneously 'le camion passant', 'the passing lorry' and 'le camion voyant', 'the seeing lorry' (Bonnet and Fieschi 1977: 27), carrying the text from the 'chambre noire' through the winter landscape waiting to be filled by the different images and stories that viewers of the film may project on to it. That the lorry functions primarily as a container for our own vision of the film is emphasised by a lengthy close-up pan of the empty cab. Driverless and without any clear direction, the lorry's meandering through the suburbs of Paris mirrors the aimless journey of the hitch-hiker who, like the 'mad' beggarwoman, has travelled far and visited many cities (Duras 1977: 46). Unrestricted by a specific identity or the ceaseless search for life's meaning, the woman in *Le Camion* is able to live fully in the present and to experience a true sense of liberation and joy. As Duras described her: 'C'est quelqu'un qui ne se demande plus rien. Elle a opéré un débarras de la recherche du sens. Elle est projetée hors d'elle, tout le temps'[30] (Bonnet and Fieschi 1977: 28). The use of the homonym 'sens' here implies that the woman is no longer looking for either meaning or direction.

30 'She is somebody who no longer asks herself any questions. She has got rid of the search for meaning. She is projected outside herself, all the time.'

Instead, she represents the process of liberation reflected in the image of the lorry whose resplendent blue colour recalls the sea and the sky as symbols of freedom in the work of Duras. Given that one of her primary concerns in *Le Camion* was to challenge the power of representation promoted both by mainstream culture and politics, it is significant that the film ends with a black image that fills the screen for sixteen seconds. While this complete absence of the image prefigures Duras's radical use of the black screen in *L'Homme Atlantique* (1981), in the late 1970s she preferred to question rather than obliterate representation.

Les Mains négatives

This eighteen-minute short is part of the block of films released in 1979 which includes *Césarée* and the two *Aurélias*. Despite evident similarities between these works, all of which use a text read by Duras's off-screen voice, there are also some important differences, in so far as *Les Mains négatives* deals with the contemporary political questions of post-colonialism and the situation of immigrant workers in French society. In this respect, the film can be seen as a further exploration of the thematics of class and race already implicit in *Le Camion*. The visual track of *Les Mains négatives* consists of a series of tracking shots filmed at dawn in the centre of Paris. This continuously moving sequence takes us from the Place de la Bastille to the Champs Elysées, via the Opéra and the majestic Parisian boulevards. Like the images in *Césarée*, these shots were originally taken for *Le Navire Night*, but later discarded as inappropriate for that particular film and used instead in *Les Mains négatives*. As with the other films in the 1979 series, the text has an apparently tenuous connection with the images, based on oblique suggestions and analogies rather than on a direct literal relationship between the images and the words heard on the soundtrack. Thus, although the film's subject matter is clearly political, the metaphorical links between sound and image create the cinematic poetry typical of Duras rather than the dry realism of more conventional political documentaries. As if to prolong the blank screen that closes *Le Camion*, *Les Mains négatives* opens with a lengthy black frame against which Duras reads the prologue of the text. In this introductory section she refers to the mysterious outlines of hands drawn in blue and black on to the walls of pre-historic caves in southern Europe.[31] These so-called 'negative hands' are the only imprint left of an ancient world which, according to the text, existed 30,000 years ago. The bare outlines of the 'negative hands' mirror not only the sketchiness of the text itself, but also the minimalist forms of representation in Duras's cinema. The main part of the text evokes a solitary pre-historic man, presumed to be the one who left the handprints in the cave and whose loneliness is underscored by Amy Flamer's discordant music, as the painfully screeching notes echo the man's screaming across the sea in his desire to communicate with others. As in *Césarée*, Duras links ancient history, or even pre-history, to twentieth-century Europe, as the text and the images of *Les Mains négatives* converge on the streets of Paris. The text/image conjunction, then, crystallises the timeless and ubiquitous dimension of Durassian cinema.

Following the film's opening sequences, our attention is increasingly drawn to the implicit correspondence between the man evoked on the soundtrack and the recurring images of immigrant workers collecting rubbish and sweeping the Parisian avenues at night. This link is first made when we see a group of refuse collectors loading up a lorry at the same time as Duras reads the following sentence from the text: 'Je suis celui qui appelait qui criait il y a trente mille ans'[32] (Duras 1979: 109). The analogy which is subsequently developed throughout the film suggests that the absence of pre-historic peoples from official recorded history is similar to the invisibility of immigrants who clean the centre of Paris in the early hours of the morning, but who disappear by 8 a.m. Paris is thus divided into two temporal and spatial dimensions, where night and darkness, representing the excluded 'other' side of French colonial and post-colonial history, fade into daylight as the white Parisians emerge in the streets and shops that have been cleaned for them by an invisible workforce. As Duras said in *Les Yeux Verts*: 'Paris à cette heure-là n'est pas à nous. Et ces gens-là, ceux qui nettoient les banques, les rues, les magasins, disparaissent complètement à huit heures, c'est alors nous qui occupons la place'[33] (Duras 1996: 124–5). This point is emphasised in the film

31 Such handprints have been discovered, in fact, in caves near Altamira in Spain.
32 'I am the one who was calling, who was shouting 30,000 years ago.'
33 'Paris at that hour doesn't belong to us. And those people, the ones who clean the banks, the streets, the shops, completely disappear at 8 a.m., and then it's us who take up the space.'

when the camera sweeps past heaps of black rubbish bags awaiting collection, as these unwanted by-products of European consumerism, hidden at night, have to disappear by early morning. The images themselves also chart this transition from night to day, as the blue of the sky becomes progressively clearer and images of white people, presumably on their way to work, begin to dominate the screen. At the same time, the sequences showing the road sweepers and refuse collectors remain in semi-darkness, underlining the social exclusion of the immigrant working class from post-colonial French society. This is strikingly conveyed when the camera brings into view a group of eight black men at a street corner, literally working in the margins of Parisian society, as they sweep up heaps of paper lying in the gutter. Dressed in identical overalls, they are perceived as an anonymous group, deprived of their individual identities, like the man in the film-text who calls for recognition of his existence. But paradoxically, the more efficiently their work is carried out, the less it is acknowledged. For, like housework, it does not generate a visible consumable product and is hence taken for granted and excluded from the official economic statistics indicating national 'productivity'. In this respect, *Les Mains négatives* recalls *Nathalie Granger*, since in both films Duras focuses on people whose work and whose very existence are usually marginalised by or, indeed, absent from mainstream society and its cinematographic representations. Duras's films, on the other hand, call on viewers to look at the margins and to see the 'otherness' behind the pretensions and façades of Western cultures. In *Les Mains négatives* the image of the negative hands, then, also becomes a metaphor for the devaluation and invisibility of the manual labour carried out by immigrants in France. But unlike the handprints in the Spanish grotto, which have survived the cataclysms of the last 30,000 years, the workers' hands leave no trace, no imprint of their lives.

Les Mains négatives, then, represents an indictment of post-colonial France which literally relegates its immigrant working class to the shadows of society, as they work in the city at night and are then forced to travel back to one of the housing estates in the suburbs filmed in *Le Camion*. The disparity between night and day in *Les Mains négatives*, with its implicit political significance, recalls Coline Serreau's popular film *Romuald et Juliette*, where Juliette also works as a cleaner at night, but at dawn returns to her council flat on the out-skirts of Paris. Duras's film, moreover, reflects the opposition between white bourgeois society and the immigrant workers in terms of the distinction between 'centre' and 'margin', both literally and metaphorically. For after the cleaners have disappeared, we are left with images of banks, cafés and shops, emblematic of the city centre which will now be taken over by the privileged classes who claim it as their space. These divisions between centre and margin, between dominant and oppressed groups, reflect not only the inequalities of contemporary French society, but also its colonial heritage. As Duras remarked, when she and her crew drove down the Parisian avenues at night to film the tracking sequences later used in *Les Mains négatives*, she was reminded of her childhood in Indochina: 'Depuis l'Indochine, depuis ma jeunesse, je n'avais jamais vu une telle population coloniale réunie dans un seul endroit. L'amour, c'est à eux qu'il s'adresse'[34] (Duras 1996: 125). This link between colonial Indochina and contemporary France also evokes the image of the beggars and lepers in *India Song* and *Son nom de Venise* who, like the immigrants of the 1970s, lived on the edges of an affluent white society. The material wealth and cultural hegemony of this society is signalled by shots of the Opéra as the icon of a bourgeois world inaccessible to the people working only a few yards down the road. And towards the end of the film the camera glides down the Champs Elysées, resting finally on a fixed frame of the Arc de Triomphe as a landmark of French imperialist and colonialist history. By contrast, the journey through Paris filmed in *Les Mains négatives* begins near the Bastille, symbolising the ideals of freedom and equality which were at the heart of the French Revolution and the subsequent Republican tradition. But while the image-track shows the monuments of a seemingly perennial history, the words spoken on the soundtrack undermine this illusory permanence, as Duras evokes the forces of nature which eventually destroy everything (Duras 1979: 113). The text/image conjunction in *Les Mains négatives* thus points to the transience of all societies, suggesting that the wealth and splendour of Paris is ultimately as precarious as that of the colonial empire which begins to crumble in *India Song* and which has already disintegrated in *Son nom de Venise*. The apocalyptic textual evocation of nature in opposition to the images of French culture recalls Duras's remark in *Les Parleuses* that the European middle classes still behave as if they and their world were immortal (Duras and Gauthier 1974:

---

34 'Since Indochina, since my youth, I'd never seen such a colonial population together in one place. My love is addressed to them.'

62–3). And yet, as the text of *Les Mains négatives* reminds us, 30,000 years ago Europe was no more than an endless wasteland (Duras 1979: 112). The primal human scream, uttered by the prehistoric man, points to the importance in Duras of archaic, 'primitive' modes of expression which have survived in the sounds and images of her own cinema and which counteract the power of language and of the visual systems of representation that divide and categorise people according to different groups and classes.

The relationship between the images and the text in '*Les Mains négatives*, then, rests on analogies as well as on a series of contrasts and oppositions. While the soundtrack invokes an archaic humanity, a pre-linguistic world of cries and screams, the visual track provides a somewhat ironic view of Western 'civilisation', as the camera lingers on the waste products of contemporary capitalism. Whereas the text inscribes the beginning of life, the image suggests the metaphorical death of contemporary European societies, already implicit in the apocalyptic landscapes of *L'Amour* (1971) and *La Femme du Gange* (1972). Likewise, the contrast between darkness and light in *Les Mains négatives* extends into the opposition between nature, evoked in the textual references to sea, wind and rocks, and the signifiers of culture, encapsulated in the film's Parisian iconography. And finally, while the text emphasises the desire for connection and relationship, the images, on the other hand, underscore the prevalent systems of social differentiation. In this context, the dichotomous relationship between text and image in *Les Mains négatives* corresponds to the hierarchical framework of binary oppositions which underpins Western culture and thought. As Hélène Cixous has shown, it is only by denying or even destroying one side of this oppositional framework that the hierarchy it supports can remain intact (Cixous and Clément 1975: 116). The continued dominance of culture, for instance, depends on the repudiation of nature, just as the privileged status of the mind and of reason entails the devaluation of the body and of the emotions. *Les Mains négatives*, however, subverts this logic. For while the image-track represents a distant and critical examination of the dominant terms, the textual track illuminates their hidden underside, the repressed foundations of Western societies, challenging the latters' claims to 'natural' superiority. In this respect, then, Duras's technique of superimposing a text read off-screen on to her images serves an implicitly political purpose in *Les Mains négatives*.

Despite Duras's overt intentions, however, it may be argued that the film implicitly reinforces colonialist and hence racist discourses. James Williams, in a critical analysis of *Les Mains négatives* suggests, for instance, that the film represents almost a denial of racism by Duras and her wish 'to return to some kind of 'prehistory', like that of the cave-paintings of "negative hands"' (Williams 1998: 81). It is true that her comparison between the fictitious prehistoric man and immigrant workers in late twentieth-century France runs the risk of disregarding the history of colonialism and of eliding differences created by specific political and historical developments through her assumptions about universally shared human experiences. And yet Duras does highlight both similarities and differences in *Les Mains négatives*, since the analogous relationships implicit in the conjunction of text and image run alongside her visual representations of the blatant social and economic disparities between the black working class and the white middle class in Paris. The ahistorical dimension of the film, then, does not necessarily justify the charge that Duras wants to contain and control racial difference by transforming the black men she filmed into the objects of her camera's gaze (Williams 1998: 84). Implicit in Williams's critique is the idea that in *Les Mains négatives* Duras reverses existing power relations with regard to both race and gender. She is thus described as the 'white, female, metropolitan writer' facing an 'objectified male other', just as the woman in the text, who is deemed to have an identity, is addressed by the anonymous man. Duras, therefore, emerges as the subject not only of the film, but also of desire, 'inscribed as totally female' (Williams 1998: 84). In my view, the construction of gender in *Les Mains négatives* is perhaps less determinate than this suggests. Although only one voice appears on the soundtrack, that of Duras herself, she speaks throughout the film from the place of a male 'I', the man in the text who is the subject of desire. As in *Le Camion* and the play *Savannah Bay* (1982), this seemingly incongruous relationship between a female voice and an imagined male speaker questions immutable gender categories. In *Les Mains négatives* this fluidity in relation to gender extends into a similar ambiguity surrounding the different representations of sexuality in the text and in the film. For instance, on the soundtrack we hear Duras, speaking from the male position, address a female object of desire when she says: 'J'appelle celle qui me répondra'.[35] In

35 'I am calling the one [the woman] who will answer me.'

the corresponding passage of the published text, by contrast, the in-determinate use of masculine and gender-neutral pronouns implies that the male 'I' could be calling out either to a man or to a woman: 'J'aimerai quiconque entendra que je crie que je t'aime'[36] (Duras 1979: 113). Through her equivocal use of language, then, Duras disrupts the distinctions between masculine and feminine subject positions, suggesting that she is not advocating a reversal of the existing gendered hierarchies, but rather the transcendence of the binary oppositions on which they hinge. Indeed, ambiguous constructions of gender and sexuality are a constant focus of her cinema, as we shall see in the final chapter.

References

Beauvoir, S. de (1976), *Le Deuxième sexe*, vol. 1, Paris, Gallimard, Collection Folio.

Bonnet, J. C. and Fieschi, J. (1977), 'Entretien avec M. Duras', *Cinématographe*, 32: 25–8.

Bouguereau, J.-M. (1990), 'Duras 89–90', *L'Evénement du jeudi*, 1–7 February, 84–7.

Cixous, H. and Clément, C. (1975), *La Jeune née*, Paris, UGE, 10/18.

Duras, M. (1973), *Nathalie Granger, suivi de La Femme du Gange*, Paris, Gallimard.

Duras, M. (1977), *Le Camion*, Paris, Minuit.

Duras, M. (1979), *Le Navire Night – Césarée – Les Mains négatives – Aurélia Steiner*, Paris, Mercure de France.

Duras, M. (1996), *Les Yeux verts*, Paris, Editions de l'Etoile/Cahiers du cinéma.

Duras. M. *et al.* (1979), *Marguerite Duras*, Paris, Editions Albatros.

Duras, M. and Gauthier, X. (1974), *Les Parleuses*, Paris, Minuit.

Duras, M. and Noguez, D. (1984), *La Classe de la violence*, interview filmed by Beaujour, J. and Mascolo, J., Le Bureau d'animation culturelle du ministère des relations extérieures.

Duras, M. and Noguez, D. (1984a), *La Dame des Yvelines*, interview, BAC.

Duras, M. and Noguez, D. (1984b), *La Caverne noir*, interview, BAC.

Duras, M. and Porte, M. (1977), *Les Lieux de Marguerite Duras*, Paris, Minuit.

Eagleton, T. (1976), *Criticism and Ideology*, London, New Left Books.

Finel-Honigman, I. (1979), '*Le Camion*: Duras's Film as Text and Process', *Revue du Pacifique*, 4(2) (Autumn), 132–43.

Forbes, J. (1992), *The Cinema in France after the New Wave*, London, MacMillan.

Garcia, I. (1981), *Promenade femmilière*, Paris, Des Femmes.

Hayward, S. (1993), *French National Cinema*, London, Routledge.

Herrmann, C. (1976), *Les Voleuses de langue*, Paris, Des Femmes.

36 'I will love whoever hears that I am shouting that I love you.'

Humm, M. (1997), *Feminism and Film*, Edinburgh, Edinburgh University Press.

Jones, A. R. (1985), 'Inscribing femininity: French theories of the feminine', in Greene, G. and Kahn, C. (eds), *Making a Difference: Feminist Literary Criticism*, London, Methuen.

Kaplan, E. A. (1983), *Women and Film: Both Sides of the Camera*, London, Methuen.

Lebelley, F. (1994), *Duras ou le poids d'une plume*, Paris, Grasset.

Mascolo, D. (1979), 'Naissance de la tragédie', in Duras, M. *et al.* (1979).

Orléan, M. (1998), 'Rétrospective: L'été Duras', *Cahiers du cinéma*, 527: 4–5.

Perrot, L. (1988), *Au-delà des pages*, no. 4, TF1.

Prédal, R. (1977), 'Le Camion: Entretien avec Marguerite Duras', *Jeune Cinéma*, 104: 16–21.

Royer, M. (1997), *L'Ecran de la passion*, Mount Nebo, Boombana Publications.

Williams, J. (1998), 'The point of no return: chiastic adventures between self and other in *Les Mains négatives* and *Au-delà des pages*', in Rodgers, C. and Udris, R. (eds), *Duras: lectures plurielles*, Amsterdam, Rodopi.

Wittig, M. (1992), *The Straight Mind and other Essays*, Hemel Hempstead, Harvester Wheatsheaf.

4

Gender and sexuality

The life and work of Duras, as we have seen, was inhabited by a multitude of tensions and ambiguities which she herself considered an essential part of her existential and creative freedom that would be stifled by entrenched political ideologies (Duras 1977: 44). In relation to her cinema, the importance of ambiguity for Duras is reflected in the representations of her female and male protagonists which reveal a characteristic discrepancy between what appears to be a specifically female film language, on the one hand, and her deconstruction of fixed gender categories, on the other. Her involvement with feminism in the early 1970s is reflected, for instance, in her indictment of the physical and psychological confinement of women in *Nathalie Granger*, where representations of the female body and of relationships between women, allied with the subversive filming of the female gaze, directly oppose patriarchal images of women by introducing a counter-cinematic model of female subjectivity. In *Nathalie Granger*, then, Duras combines the feminist ideas inscribed into the film narrative with a female film language reflected in her cinematographic technique. But although this apparently gender-specific quality of Durassian cinema is clearly perceptible in this film, the latter also shows a certain progression towards the deconstruction of gendered identities in *India Song* and, even more prominently, in *Agatha*.

The preoccupation in Duras with questions of gender and sexuality may be usefully theorised by drawing on ideas central to feminist psychoanalysis. Although both feminism and psychoanalysis have lost the central position they occupied among the various approaches to film studies in the 1970s, in relation to Durassian cinema they can still be seen as valuable conceptual tools, particularly in the context of the work of the French psychoanalyst Jacques Lacan and the adaptation of his ideas to feminist theory. Prominent among these are the Lacanian concepts of the Imaginary and the Symbolic order which will be briefly explained here and which will be used in subsequent analyses in this chapter.[1] In Lacan's theory of human psychosexual development, the Imaginary is the stage in early childhood where all infants of both sexes relate most closely to their mothers who represent the centre of their world. During the Imaginary, the almost fusional union of the mother/child dyad prevails over separation and differentiation, as the infant has not yet acquired a separate sense of self nor an understanding of the different social categories of identity, including gender identity. At this stage, therefore, the child is unaware of the complex social norms and expectations linked to gender and grafted on to biological sex. However, the mother/child relationship comes to an end through the intervention of the father who represents the position of authority in the patriarchal Symbolic order. It must be noted that 'the father' in Lacan is an abstract figure representing the paternal law in patriarchal societies and not the individual father of a particular family.[2] Most importantly, from a feminist point of view, the intervention of the Law-of-the-Father entails the repression of the earlier Imaginary stage of experience and thus, as Luce Irigaray has put it, 'the obliteration of the mother' to ensure the continued hegemony of patriarchal society (Irigaray 1994: 13). As a result of this transition from the maternal Imaginary to the paternal Symbolic order, the child is obliged to take up her or his allotted place in the social system of gender identities by learning the prescribed 'masculine' or 'feminine' modes of being. However, as Kaplan has pointed out, because of the hierarchical organisation of patriarchy, girls are assigned the place of the female object in the Symbolic order, while boys are able to take up their position as male subjects by identifying with the authority held by the father (Kaplan 1983: 26).

One of the central concerns of feminist film theory was to show how the sexual inequalities inherent in patriarchal societies are reflected in their cultural formations, for example in mainstream cinema. Thus, as Judith Mayne has pointed out, Hollywood cinema is

1 The capitalisation of these terms is a commonly used convention which draws attention to their specific meanings in Lacanian theory.
2 For a more detailed discussion of the Imaginary and the Symbolic, see Turkle, 1979.

constructed around the oppositions between men and women, subjects and objects, seeing and being seen that provide the foundation of the Symbolic order (Mayne 1990: 21). Films directed by women, on the other hand, often deconstruct this dichotomous framework and instead evoke a world 'prior to or outside the realm of the Symbolic order' (Mayne 1990: 150). This comment is certainly appropriate to the cinema of Duras, as the centrality of her female protagonists and the 'feminised' representations of some of the male figures reflect her desire to question the binary gender categories of patriarchy and to recreate the fluid indistinct domain of the Imaginary. And given that, in patriarchal cultures, gender differences are represented primarily in visual terms, the use of disembodied voices in her later films affirms the destruction of gender identity through the primacy of the voice over the image. While the creation of a female counter-cinema in *Nathalie Granger* enabled Duras to question dominant structures of representation, ultimately her films went beyond the dichotomies of gender and sexuality. In her cinema Duras used her characteristic blending and blurring of voices, sounds and images to demolish the essentialist idea that gendered identities arise 'naturally' from anatomical sex differences. Furthermore, her deconstruction of the assumed antithesis between 'masculine' and 'feminine' identities also challenges the patriarchal model of heterosexuality as the only acceptable model of human sexual expression, based on the perception of men and women as 'opposites'. In Durassian cinema, on the contrary, the relationships of identification and proximity that prevail in the Imaginary form the basis of sexual desire, regardless of the biological sex of her protagonists. This link between identification and desire, severed by the child's entry into the Symbolic order, breaks down the foundations of patriarchal cinema, disrupting what Mayne has called 'the fit between the hierarchies of masculinity and femininity [...] and activity and passivity' (Mayne 1990: 118). Given that this 'fit' is also an essential aspect of the prevalent model of heterosexuality, Duras's challenge to binary oppositions introduces a certain homoerotic current into her cinema. Viewers of her films, then, are left without a 'clearly marked place' (Mayne 1990: 129), as they can no longer comfortably identify with the conventional positions assigned to men and women in mainstream cinema. Instead, like Duras's protagonists, the spectator is invited to revisit the Imaginary and, therefore, her or his original bisexuality.

Nathalie Granger

As suggested in the previous chapter, *Nathalie Granger* may be read at (at least) two different levels. Although, on the one hand, the film implicitly reproduces the conventional constructions of gender by creating separate 'masculine' and 'feminine' spheres, on the other hand, we can see Duras beginning to question and deconstruct all gender categories. This process may be traced through her representations of three central relationships in the film: the relationship between Nathalie and her mother; the friendship between Isabelle and *l'Amie* (the Friend); and, finally, the two encounters between the women and the washing-machine salesman, played by the then relatively unknown Gérard Depardieu starring in his first film. These three relationships, as we shall see, chart a progression in Durassian cinema from a universe based on clearly delineated categories of gender and sexuality to a world in which shared experiences transcend the constraints of gender. Crucial in this process of transformation is the theme of violence which, although never explicitly represented, runs through the entire film.

This implicit, yet all-pervasive violence, is associated mainly with the two young murderers who, according to the regular news flashes on the radio, are hiding from the police in the forest at Dreux, and Nathalie herself who has apparently hit another pupil at school and whose headmistress repeatedly voices her misgivings about what she perceives as Nathalie's abnormal behaviour, 'cette violence chez une petite fille', 'such violence in a little girl'. Although, in typically Durassian fashion, the reasons for this violence are never clearly stated, we may nevertheless assume that they are linked to Nathalie's rebellion against her mother and, by extension, the society which the latter represents. The conflict between mother and daughter is conveyed through the different locations in the film, since we usually see Nathalie in the park, connecting her to the youngsters in the forest by situating her beyond the perimeters of 'civilised' society. Isabelle, by contrast, is associated primarily with the traditionally 'feminine', prison-like environment of the house. Nathalie's violent insubordination, then, can be seen as an expression of the girl's revolt both against the idea that femininity is synonymous with meek obedience and against her mother whose submissiveness in the early parts of the film conforms to such conventional gender codes. While Nathalie externalises her anger and frustration, Isabelle passively accepts her own disempowerment and even colludes with the demands of the patriarchal order by agreeing to send her daughter to a school for 'unstable' children: 'Nathalie doit aller,'*disent-ils*, à la pension Datkin afin qu'on soigne la violence dont elle est atteinte'[3] (Duras 1973: 29). Playing the role of the typically 'feminine' woman, devoid of identity and autonomy, Isabelle Granger may be seen as a victim of patriarchal violence who nevertheless perpetuates that violence by directing it both at herself, in the form of mental illness, and at Nathalie who suffers the effects of her mother's emotional unavailability. Throughout the film, Isabelle's distance in relation to the child is mirrored in Nathalie's introverted withdrawal from the world, suggesting that her violence is at least partly a defence against her mother's apparent indifference towards her. Indeed, Isabelle, and even more so her friend, seem to prefer Laurence, Nathalie's elder sister, who resembles the friend to such an extent that viewers of the film might initially assume that they are, in fact, mother and daughter. Nathalie, on the other hand, takes after Isabelle, both physically and in terms of their similar personalities, 'isolées dans une violence de même nature, sauvage: celle de l'amour, celle du refus'[4] (Duras 1973: 69). Both victim and oppressor, Isabelle Granger projects her own suffering on to Nathalie who has become a mirror image of her mother. Ultimately, as Kaplan has noted, the tension between mother and daughter in *Nathalie Granger* reflects not so much an individual conflict as the disastrous effects of women's physical and emotional confinement in patriarchal societies (Kaplan 1983: 97).

However, if the mother/daughter relationship in *Nathalie Granger* highlights the psychological consequences of women's oppression, it also heralds the possibility of their liberation and with it a radical transformation of all human relationships. This ambiguity in the film's narrative and thematic structure is encapsulated in the conjunction between music and violence that pervades the entire film. Music in *Nathalie Granger*, as in Duras's 1958 novel *Moderato cantabile*, becomes an instrument of social repression which, in both works, manifests itself through the controlling behaviour of mothers towards their children. Like the little boy in *Moderato cantabile*, Nathalie is

---

3 'Nathalie must go to the Datkin boarding school, *they keep saying*, so that the violence that afflicts her can be treated.'

4 'isolated in the same untamed violence: the violence of love, of refusal'

forced to take piano lessons by Isabelle who, in the absence of the girl's father, comes to represent the values of a patriarchal middle-class education system. After Mr Granger has left the house, for instance, Isabelle rings the 'special' school to which Nathalie will be sent, insisting that her daughter continue to learn the piano. Her claim to authority, however, is refuted by Duras herself, whose voice at the other end of the telephone confirms the child's freedom of choice: 'CE SERA A NATHALIE ELLE-MEME DE CHOISIR DE FAIRE OU NON DU PIANO'[5] (Duras 1973: 20). But, while music is clearly an expression of maternal control, the piano also comes to symbolise Isabelle's own loss of freedom and artistic creativity, suggested by the fact that, although she was once an accomplished musician, she is no longer able to play the piano. This experience of loss and despair is conden-sed in the scene where Isabelle sits down at the piano, but is unable to play as her hands fall into her lap in a gesture of despondency. From this point onwards, however, music becomes increasingly associated with women's revolt against the violence of social control. Thus, following the piano teacher's departure in the latter half of the film, the music expresses Nathalie's violence (Duras 1973: 74) and signals Isabelle's act of revolt at the end of the film when her repressed anger finally erupts. The music in *Nathalie Granger*, then, signifies conflict and alienation in the mother/daughter relationship as well as the increasing affinity and complicity between Isabelle and Nathalie. As Kaplan has suggested, the music may be interpreted as a signifier of the pre-linguistic world of the Imaginary, in contrast with the domin-ance of language in the patriarchal Symbolic order (Kaplan 1983: 98). The growing bond between mother and daughter, following the piano lesson, does suggest a return to the realm of the maternal, under-scored by Isabelle's decision not to send her daughter to the 'remedial' school. The mother's refusal to subject her daughter to the rigid discipline of society is mirrored in one of the film's closing shots where we see Nathalie in her bedroom, curled up in the foetal position as if to emphasise the bond which now connects her to her mother.

In *Nathalie Granger* both music and the female gaze convey women's attempts at creating a sense of solidarity that would over-come their distance and isolation from one another in patriarchal societies. The female gaze in Durassian cinema implies a visual

5 'It'll be up to Nathalie herself to choose whether or not she wants to play the piano' (in capitals in the text).

gesturing towards the other which directly counteracts the power of the male gaze in mainstream film. In *Nathalie Granger* this different way of looking is particularly poignant in the triangular scene at the pond, where the camera focuses on Nathalie, as she looks at Laurence and the friend who are cleaning the pond and witnesses their affectionate relationship from which she is excluded. The proximity and emotional intimacy between Laurence and the friend is suggested by their physical resemblance, highlighted not only by their blond hair, but also by the fact that both are wearing black trousers. Their closeness contrasts painfully with Nathalie's loneliness and aliena-tion, mirrored in that of her mother who stands behind Nathalie, secretly observing her child. This scene clearly deconstructs the classic masculine gaze built into patriarchal cinema which typically positions viewers in such a way that they are forced to identify with the male hero looking at women. If the hero is normally the subject of the film's action and narrative, the female characters are often no more than the objects of his gaze.[6] By contrast, as this scene demonstrates, Duras aligns the spectator's perspective with the female gaze, as we are invited to look *with* Nathalie and Isabelle, not *at* them. This is emphasised by the fact that, here as elsewhere in *Nathalie Granger*, the actresses are filmed from behind, so that the spectator is obliged to follow the trajectory of their gaze and, therefore, to adopt the female subject position. Duras's film, then, creates a relationship of identi-fication rather than of voyeurism between its spectators and its female protagonists. As we are looking at women who have themselves become the subject rather than the object of the gaze, the patriarchal boundaries between male and female, subject and object begin to disintegrate. In the scene in question, furthermore, Duras begins to challenge the heterosexual construction of the gaze in mainstream cinema by filming women looking at women. But, unlike the objecti-fying male gaze, the exchange of looks between Nathalie and Isabelle expresses their longing for closeness and inclusion, as they try to go beyond the divisions among women within the Symbolic order.[7] Given that women have been excluded from both the dominant culture and language, it is perhaps not surprising that in Duras their initial efforts to communicate with one another are visual rather than

6 For more on the gendered dichotomy of the gaze in mainstream narrative cinema, see Mulvey, 1975.

7 For a more detailed discussion of this subject, see Irigaray, 1977.

verbal, as looking seems to replace talking throughout much of the film. The female gaze as a form of silent communication becomes particularly poignant during the piano lesson, when Isabelle looks at Nathalie through the window in a way that suggests her longing to be reunited with her daughter, 'privée de cette enfant, dans la faim de cette enfant, enfermée'[8] (Duras 1973: 72–3). Indeed, her 'violent' gesture at the end of the film expresses both her revolt against the destructiveness of society and her solidarity with Nathalie, undermining the patriarchal norms of femininity that had imprisoned Isabelle herself in the earlier sections of the film.

Nathalie Granger, then, charts a certain progression in its representation of the mother/daughter relationship from an initial hostility and mutual distance to the growing proximity between Isabelle and Nathalie. This tacit female complicity is even more noticeable in the filming of the relationship between Isabelle and her friend, as Duras subverts the conventional model of female relationships, according to which women are perceived as enemies and rivals, competing for male attention. In *Nathalie Granger* such destructive stereotypes are countered by the affectionate bond that characterises the friendship between Isabelle and the friend. Indeed, the female relationship takes centre stage in the film, since Isabelle's husband remains a marginal figure, while the travelling salesman becomes the women's accomplice in their challenge to society rather than an object of potential rivalry between them. The theme of female solidarity against a hostile society is condensed from the beginning of the film in the image of Nathalie's headmistress talking to two women, assumed to be Isabelle and her friend. This shot is then repeated at several points in the film, emphasising the friend's constant support for both Isabelle and Nathalie who are struggling, in different ways, with the demands of a repressive social order. Aware of Isabelle's illness and of her difficult relationship with Nathalie, the friend offers to let the girl stay with her on Saturdays, once she has been sent to the boarding school. Replacing Isabelle in her maternal role, moreover, she fetches Nathalie and her sister from school and makes sandwiches for them. Although in the early parts of the film Duras emphasises the emotional affinity that unites Isabelle and the friend, she also highlights the differences between them in a number of visual sequences. For instance, the

8 'deprived of this child, yearning for this child, trapped'

close-up shots of the women's hands clearing the table after lunch draw attention to Isabelle's hesitant clumsy gestures, by comparison with her friend's dexterity when she picks up the glasses and crockery and carries them to the kitchen. A similar distinction is noticeable between Isabelle's slow, awkward gait, as she walks around the house, and the other woman's agile movements when she collects branches in the garden. The fact that, at the beginning of *Nathalie Granger*, Isabelle is dressed in black and is filmed exclusively inside the house associates her with the theme of imprisonment and oppression, whereas the friend, often seen outside and wearing lighter colours, embodies the sense of liberation that permeates the closing sections of the film. The scene where she makes a fire in the garden further strengthens her association with the film's underlying passion and energy which is initially lacking in Isabelle. Thus, if the latter epitomises the archetypal model of patriarchal femininity, since she seems passively resigned to her fate, her friend, on the other hand, represents female subjectivity and self-affirmation. While Isabelle directs her anger against herself, in the form of depression, the friend openly expresses it, for example when she phones the *préfecture* to protest against the unjust treatment of her Portuguese housekeeper Maria who, because she is unable to read French, has unwittingly signed her own expulsion from France. The friend's revolt against this injustice is visually conveyed in the scene immediately following the telephone call, where we see Jeanne Moreau's face in a mirror, her eyes ablaze with anger. The violence inficed on Isabelle and Maria who, as women and as foreigners, are both alienated from a patriarchal French society, creates the potential for counter-violence, since the women's repressed anger is gradually externalised and turned against that society.

Throughout *Nathalie Granger*, the differences between the two women alternate with patterns of similarities, to the extent where the representations of Isabelle and the friend are virtually mirror images of each other. This oscillation between sameness and difference in the film's central female relationship has a direct bearing on its constructions and deconstructions of gender and sexuality as an integral part of its thematic framework. Thus, on the one hand, the female protagonists in *Nathalie Granger* replicate the traditional binary model of gendered behaviour, since Isabelle confirms the norm of passive femininity while her friend epitomises the active energy typically associated with masculinity in patriarchal cultures. On the other hand, however, Duras undermines these oppositional representations through a number of visual sequences where the differences between the two female figures become blurred. By accentuating their physical and emotional affinity, moreover, Duras effectively questions not only conventional perceptions of gender, but also the dominant heterosexual model of relationships, since the affectionate friendship between women introduces an underlying lesbian dimension into the film. Duras dismantles existing boundaries of gender and sexuality through what we might call the intersubjective female gaze and through the way in which she films the similarities between the two women's postures and movements. The repeated sequences showing Isabelle and her friend looking at each other convey the sense of mutual empathy inherent in their friendship, as the spectator sees the women from each other's point of view and not from the perspective of the voyeuristic camera that is usually aligned with the eye of a male protagonist. The bond between the two women is emphasised, furthermore, by the repeated shots of Bose and Moreau sitting next to each other below a mirror. The women's static postures in these shots are symmetrical, yet not identical, emphasising both the differences and the similarities between them. The mirror is used here as a visual metaphor for the mutual identification between the female characters which may also include the spectator, whether male or female. For, as Mayne has remarked, the figure of the mirror breaks down the oppositions between male and female, active and passive, viewer and viewed, since it reflects the ambiguous image of another who is different from but also similar to the self (Mayne 1990: 89). This fusion between self and other is implicit in the figure of the twin or double to which Duras alluded in' *Les Parleuses* when she compared the house inhabited by Isabelle and the friend to a kind of inter-uterine space and described the two female figures as floating in the same liquid (Duras and Gauthier 1974: 73). This comment not only emphasises the identificatory nature of the relationship between the two women, but also reinforces their link with the maternal sphere of the Imaginary, symbolised by the womb-like enclosure of the house. As Irigaray has argued, the survival of the patriarchal Symbolic order depends upon the radical separation between women, as they are forced into 'exile' from their original relationship with their mothers (Irigaray 1974: 48). In *Nathalie Granger*, on the contrary, the emotional affinity between Isabelle and the friend suggests not only a return to this forbidden female territory, but also the fact that their growing sense of solidarity heralds their incipient revolt against society. In terms of the film narrative, Isabelle's proximity to and increasing resemblance with her friend signals her transformation, as she becomes more active, reclaiming both her own life and her relationship with her daughter. This metamorphosis begins when Isabelle goes into the garden to help her friend make a fire. In this scene Isabelle expresses her desire for freedom since, for the first time in the film, she leaves the claustrophobic environment of the house and ventures into the open space outside. Similarly, she now plays a more active role, as she helps her friend collect wood and puts some branches on the fire. The fire as a metaphor of the film's underlying violence is replicated later when Isabelle throws the shredded remnants of *Le Monde* and the letter from the electricity board into the blazing coal fire. In visual terms, this subversion of the patriarchal model of femininity is conveyed through the association between the women and the fire, a conventional symbol of masculine action and energy. Indeed, the metaphorical significance of the fire contrasts with the traditionally feminine symbolism of water, captured in the repeated background images of the pond, its surface reflecting the Granger house. At the same time as Duras challenges the gendered oppositions between 'masculine' and 'feminine' behaviour by aligning both her female characters with active subjectivity, she also emphasises the silent complicity between Isabelle and the other woman. Given that the conventional construction of heterosexual relationships relies on binary gender divisions, the central female relationship in *Nathalie Granger* provides an alternative to this dominant model, one that is based on mutual empathy and reciprocity. In visual terms this intersubjective relationship is constructed through the women's physical proximity, as they are filmed standing next to each other in front of the fire. When the friend returns to the garden, having gone into the house to answer the telephone, we see the two women walking towards each other, and as Isabelle puts a cardigan round her friend's shoulders, their bodies seem to merge within the frame, representing what Owen Heathcote has aptly described as 'a symbiotic female ballet' (Heathcote 2000: 80). The implicit homoeroticism of this shot is unusual in filmic representations of female relationships and certainly militates against the more familiar heterosexual images of 'bitchy' women. In *Nathalie Granger*, Moreau and Bose are clearly not acting to either a male director or an imaginary male audience and can, therefore, dissociate themselves from the spectacle of patriarchal femininity that actresses are expected to stage in mainstream cinema. In Duras's film, on the other hand, even Isabelle Granger, initially typecast in the feminine role, is able to break out of the traditional mould, affirming the feminist view that gender identities are socially constructed and not preordained by biological sex. As Mayne has remarked, the lesbian undercurrent in films made by women directors dissolves the asymmetrical dualistic framework underlying dominant perceptions of both gender and sexuality (Mayne 1990: 118). Instead, the way in which Duras films her two female protagonists constructs a relationship based on equality and symmetry, both in the scene showing Isabelle and the friend in the garden and in a later sequence where, immediately after their visit to Nathalie's headmistress, they are sitting opposite each other at the kitchen table in the Granger house, their exchange of glances and smiles hinting at their shared understanding: 'Elles se regardent. Se sourient. Cessent de se regarder. Sourire très doux: elles sourient à leur angoisse ... Complicité vertigineuse entre les deux femmes'[9] (Duras 1973: 42). The tenderness implicit in the smile and the looks mirrors the physical closeness of the previous scene and reinforces the powerful sense of complicity that underpins Duras's representation of female relationships in *Nathalie Granger*.

The film's exclusively female environment, however, is transformed with the appearance in the Granger household of the anonymous salesman whose presence introduces a typically Durassian triangle, made up of one male and two female protagonists and which is already familiar to readers of *Dix Heures et demie du soir en été* (1960), *Le Ravissement de Lol V. Stein* (1964) and *Détruire dit-elle* (1969). In *Nathalie Granger*, however, as in *Détruire dit-elle*, the emotional bond between the female characters undercuts the potential for female animosity and rivalry inherent in the conventional structure of triangular heterosexual relationships. By contrast with the latter, the two encounters in *Nathalie Granger* between the man and the women function as a key mechanism through which Duras continues to subvert conventional representations of both gender and sexuality,

9 'They look at each other. Smile at each other. Stop looking at each other. A very gentle smile: they smile at their anguish ... Breathtaking complicity between the two women.'

using the visual strategies of reversal and ambiguity in relation to the spectator's expectations concerning gendered forms of behaviour and interaction.

That the filming of the salesman's encounter with the women undermines dominant constructions of gender is implicit from the moment he enters the Grangers' living room. Throughout the entire visit, Duras uses the classic shot–reverse shot sequence, in which the camera's focus oscillates between the man and the two women, whereas the previous sequences invariably represent the female protagonists in the same frame. This startling change in the film's visual discourse is significant in relation to gender. For while the physical juxtaposition of the two women highlights their similarities, the film's particular use of the shot–reverse shot sequence suggests a reversal of the masculine and feminine positions inscribed in the visual codes of mainstream patriarchal cinema. If, as Kaja Silverman has argued, the classic shot–reverse shot technique 'aligns the female body with the male gaze' (Silverman 1988: 28), its subversive adaptation by Duras has the opposite effect, as in *Nathalie Granger* it is the male body that is subjected to the scrutiny of the two women's fixed impassive gaze. Contrary to both social norms and dominant filmmaking practices, the man in Duras's film initially becomes the object of the female gaze and the target of the women's silent hostility, as they gradually undermine his confidence in an attempt to break down his false social persona. The verbal negation of the man's social identity, repeated three times in the film by Jeanne Moreau, implies that his self-definition in terms of his occupation denies his individual existence. Thus the statement 'VOUS N'ETES PAS VOYAGEUR DE COMMERCE'[10] both highlights and criticises the travelling salesman's efforts to adopt an identity that merely imitates a certain middle-class model of patriarchal masculinity. This inauthentic self, both in terms of class and gender, is clearly perceptible in Duras's visual construction of her male protagonist throughout this sequence. The false assurance of his gestures is as rehearsed as the script he recites in front of the women, repeatedly pointing at them to underline the 'truth' of his statements about the 'vendetta tambour' (washing machine). The didactic index finger and the self-satisfied, knowledgeable smile as he instructs them on the technical merits of the machine, are part

10 'YOU ARE NOT A TRAVELLING SALESMAN' (in capitals in the text).

of a Durassian parody of his pretence of masculine superiority, as he advises and informs the two supposedly 'ignorant' women. The latter, however, refuse to play their allotted part in this scenario, as their unwillingness to respond to the salesman's talk undercuts the viewer's expectations with regard to conventional male–female interactions in cinema. However, just as the women reject their socially prescribed feminine identities, the salesman's masculinity soon turns out to be a superficial façade which begins to crumble as he becomes visibly more and more nervous and disconcerted by the women's underlying animosity towards him. As Michelle Royer has rightly pointed out, in *Nathalie Granger* women are both victims of patriarchal oppression and oppressors in turn (Royer 1997: 85). It is true that the psychological violence inflicted on the man by the women is almost unbearable in parts of this sequence, particularly when their denial of his masculine persona transforms him into a defenceless child, facing two stern maternal figures. At this point, the visual coding of the salesman's gender identity is counteracted by a series of gestures which conveys his vulnerability, as he clutches his briefcase in search of comfort, nervously licking his lips and looking down instead of gazing directly at the women. However, although the latter's callousness may strike a discordant note in the film's audiences, it is important to stress that, for Duras, violence was often a necessary means of breaking down oppressive and alienating social identities, in particular those pertaining to gender and class. If, as Irigaray has argued, women in patriarchal societies are obliged to participate in a 'masquerade of femininity' and to 'mime' male discourse (Irigaray 1977: 131, 74), the male protagonist in *Nathalie Granger* who is 'disguised as a salesman', imitates not only the language of the bosses, but also that of the patriarchal Symbolic order (Duras 1973: 52, 54). The women's psychological violence, then, can be seen as a liberating force, since it explodes false identities and ultimately frees both the salesman and the women themselves from their 'être social', 'their social being' (Duras 1973: 79). At the same time, the salesman's first encounter with the women clearly demonstrates that gendered identities are not biologically predetermined. Instead, as Judith Butler has shown, expressions of gender become dramatised like a performance, depending on certain learned behaviours which are imposed upon and which subsequently divide men and women into two radically distinct groups (see Butler 1990). The notion of gender as performance is clearly relevant to

Nathalie Granger, as Depardieu's slightly exaggerated gestures and facial expressions constantly remind us not only that he is an actor, but also that the male figure he represents is acting out the role of the salesman as part of this gendered spectacle. The sharp contrast, furthermore, between the man's initially confident performance and his subsequent vulnerability in front of the women also foregrounds this discrepancy between his spurious masculinity and the fundamental humanity he shares with Isabelle and her friend. It is evident, then, that the women's implicit violence is not directed at the man personally, but rather at a society that imposes such rigid prescriptions of gendered behaviour on a multitude of different individuals. This is substantiated in the film by the fact that, towards the end of his first visit, the man begins to agree with the women's rejection of social definitions, including that of his own phoney identity as a salesman (Duras 1973: 59). His inability to sustain his masculine performance, moreover, is an essential aspect of his position in the film, since it is only because of his underlying 'femininity' that he is eventually able to join the women, as they extend the complicity between them to include the man as well. As Duras remarked in the postscript of the text *Nathalie Granger*: '*Homme pour rire*: c'est ce que penseraient les autres hommes de lui, les "vrais" ... L'homme du film est donc un homme que les autres hommes refuseraient mais que les femmes acceuillent'[11] (Duras 1973: 91).

The salesman's first visit to the Granger house ends with his suggestion that he might like to meet the two women again: 'Si vous voulez ... je repasserai dans un mois'[12] (Duras 1973: 60). The tentative quality of this utterance, inviting the women's agreement, indicates that, as the man is no longer constrained by his masculine persona, he may now be able to engage in a more reciprocal relationship with his female counterparts. His transformation seems complete when, at the end of his visit, he is on the verge of tears, his emotional, 'feminine' side contrasting with the bogus toughness of his previous 'masculine' identity. The man's affinity with the two women dissolves not only the binary divisions of gender, but also the dominant definitions of sexuality which depend on perceptions of 'difference' or

11 '*A man to laugh at*: that's what the other men would think of him, the "real" ones ... The man in the film is a man who would be rejected by other men but welcomed by women.'
12 'If you like, I'll drop in again in a month.'

'sameness' in relation to sex and gender. Because Duras blurs the boundaries between these categories, it is no longer possible to define the relationships in *Nathalie Granger* as either 'heterosexual' or 'homosexual'. As Heathcote has put it: 'By showing sexuality to be defined and represented in terms of permeable positionalities, Duras shows sexuality to be infinitely fluid and exchangeable' (Heathcote 2000: 80). That this fluidity has replaced the rigid gender positions in patriarchal societies is suggested by the fact that Duras no longer uses the shot–reverse shot technique to film the salesman's second visit. Instead when he talks to Isabelle during this sequence, both of them are contained within the same shot, as they sit together at the kitchen table, recalling the symmetrical postures that visually connect the female protagonists in earlier parts of the film. Furthermore, the sense of reciprocity and recognition implicit in the exchange of looks and in the dialogue between Isabelle and the anonymous man reinforces the fact that the gendered oppositions of the patriarchal Symbolic order have now disappeared and that the man and the woman can, therefore, relate to each other as authentic human beings. If the man is no longer limited by his masculine posturing, Isabelle, in turn, has finally freed herself from the shackles of patriarchal femininity, since she has asserted her own wishes by refusing to send her child to the remedial school. The mutual empathy that now links the man and the women is confirmed when the friend appears in the door frame, smiling at the stories he tells about his previous jobs. At the end of the film, then, Duras transcends the barriers of both gender and class by creating a relationship of mutual understanding between a working-class man and two middle-class women. The oppositional categories of the Symbolic order become irrelevant, as the man reconnects with his 'femininity', just as the women's anger and violence are an expression of their 'masculinity'. As Bonita Oliver has remarked: 'Il [l'homme] redevient cet être bissexué dont parle Freud et que chacun de nous est en naissant'[13] (Oliver 1985: 37). This process of transformation, through which Duras charts her protagonists' return to their original 'bisexual' state begins with *Nathalie Granger*, but asserts its presence even more clearly in *India Song*.

---

13 'He [the man] reverts back to the bisexual nature that Freud talks about and that we all share at birth.'

India Song

In *La Couleur des mots*, a series of interviews about *India Song*, Duras emphasised the crucial importance of Anne-Marie Stretter who, during her childhood, became a substitute for her own, emotionally unavailable mother and who subsequently occupied centre stage in several books and films. Duras's recreation of Anne-Marie Stretter in all these works, particularly in *India Song*, however, transcends the purely autobiographical dimension and instead immerses her viewers in an archetypal maternal presence which pervades the entire film. In terms of feminist psychoanalytical theory, *India Song* questions the categories of gender and sexuality constructed by the patriarchal Symbolic order by foregrounding the Imaginary. The return journey from the Symbolic to the Imaginary traced by the film necessarily implies a blurring of the boundaries between 'masculine' and 'feminine', 'heterosexual' and 'homosexual', since these divisions only occur after the child's transition from the original maternal sphere to the patriarchal order. Thus, it is perhaps the film's underlying deconstruction of all fixed categories of identity that strikes such a powerful chord in its spectators, as *India Song* leads us back to the archaic repressed memories of our origins.

The importance of the mother in *India Song* is apparent from the film's opening section where the long shot of the sunset is accompanied by the beggarwoman's song, sung in her mother tongue.[14] This initial reference is reinforced in the subsequent sequence, as we listen to the theme tune of *India Song*, at the same time as the camera lingers on Anne-Marie Stretter's piano, Duras's symbolic shrine to her heroine and hence, by implication, to the mother (Porte 1983: 56). Both sound and image in the film, then, evoke the presence of its female figures in terms of their shared association with the Imaginary and the maternal, which undermines the patriarchal construction of 'the feminine' by comparison with and in opposition to 'the masculine'. If, in classical Freudian theory, women are defined according to their 'difference' from men, *India Song* presents us with an alternative framework that represents women in terms of their closeness to the mother and, by extension, to other women. The emphasis in the film

---

14 For an excellent analysis of the maternal in relation to the use of song in cinema, see Geraldine Walsh-Harrington, 1999.

on relations of proximity or contiguity subverts the patriarchal preoccupation with definitions of identity and difference and underlines
instead the connectedness between people and phenomena. This is
particularly striking in the sequence of metonymic close-up shots
which follows the initial appearance on the soundtrack of the theme
tune of *India Song* and which represents a number of objects associated with Anne-Marie Stretter, for instance her dress and her jewellery. At first glance, this sequence looks like a classic example of
fetishism, discussed at length by Mulvey and other feminist film
theorists whose work has been influenced by Freudian psychoanalysis.[15] According to these theorists, the obsessive visual focus in
patriarchal cinema on parts of the female body or objects associated
with it can be seen to mitigate the 'threat of castration' that women on
screen may pose to the male spectator (Mulvey 1975: 199). Although
fetishism does play an important part in the visual representation of
Anne-Marie Stretter, Duras subverts the dominant meanings associated with this filmic device. Instead of functioning as a way of recon-
structing patriarchal images of women as inferior, 'castrated' versions
of men, Duras's use of fetishism strengthens the link between the
feminine and the maternal and thus erodes the ideological foundations
of the Symbolic order. Indeed, as Kaplan has remarked, the masculine focus on the female threat of castration, both in psychoanalyis
and in film theory, is probably 'designed to mask an even greater
threat that mothering poses' (Kaplan 1984: 334). In *India Song*, then,
because of Anne-Marie Stretter's relationship with the maternal, the
fetishised objects associated with her function as substitutes for the
Imaginary mother, repressed by patriarchy in order to maintain the
position of power occupied by the Symbolic father. Thus, when the
vice-consul touches Anne-Marie Stretter's red bicycle, he expresses
his desire not only to be united with the woman herself, but also to
return to the maternal space she represents in the film. This subversive use of fetishistic images in *India Song* is most evident in the
unusually long close-up shot of Delphine Seyrig's breast. It is clear
that Duras deliberately filmed this shot in a way that was designed to
question dominant representations of women's breasts as objects of
male sexual desire. In this image, on the contrary, the breast is shown
as part of a living female body, as our attention is drawn to the

15 See Mulvey, 1975 and Silverman, 1988.

woman's breathing and perspiration. Moreover, as Duras herself pointed out, since Delphine Seyrig was breastfeeding her son during the making of *India Song*, this shot also highlights the nurturing and life-giving function of the breast and gives it a sense of dignity that is generally lacking in patriarchal representations of the female body (Duras 1979: 86). Equally surprising here is the conjunction between the soundtrack and the visual track, as the close-up image of Seyrig is accompanied by a litany of place names, uttered by the two female voices. While these names evidently refer to the Asian cities that Anne-Marie Stretter visited with her husband, they also recall the beggarwoman's itinerary from Savannakhet to Calcutta. In this way, the film creates a further parallel between these two female figures, as the image of the breast comes to symbolise women's shared experience of exile and dislocation from their origins in patriarchal cultures. Paradoxically, then, in *India Song* Duras uses fetishistic images precisely in order to undermine the familiar constructions of patriarchal femininity in mainstream cinema. Thus, while Anne-Marie Stretter displays all the emblems of the seductive 'femme fatale', such as the low-cut red or black dress and the red hair, these visual signifiers are not associated with the conventional characterisation of the woman as the simultaneously seductive and destructive 'temptress'. On the contrary, the figure of Anne-Marie Stretter appears rather self-effacing and unobtrusive, affectionate rather than overtly sexual towards the men around her, as she simultaneously stages and undercuts the fantasy of the 'femme fatale'.

The subversion in *India Song* of the dominant visual codes of femininity is extended to a deconstruction of patriarchal masculinity, most importantly through Duras's representations of the vice-consul as the film's central male figure. This is already implicit in the vice-consul's first appearance, as we see him walking by a lake in the park of the embassy gardens. The implicit association created here between the vice-consul and the traditionally 'feminine' element of water, as we see his reflection in the lake, prefigures the subsequent chain of identifications between the male protagonist and the female figures of the beggarwoman and Anne-Marie Stretter. These feminine identifications underpin the entire film, challenging the oppositional patterns of gendered identities that structure more conventional film narratives. The gender ambiguities surrounding the figure of the vice-consul are foregrounded, moreover, by the fact that he is dressed in white, conventionally associated with the 'feminine' characteristics of purity and virginity, confirmed by the off-screen female voices who describe him as 'l'homme vierge de Lahore', 'the virginal man from Lahore'. This feminising representation of the vice-consul, however, contrasts with his evidently masculine features, such as his tall stature, his full beard and Michael Lonsdale's deep voice. Duras's construction of her male protagonist, then, exemplifies her dismantling of sharply drawn gender boundaries and hence her desire to abolish patriarchal gender divisions by focusing on experiences common to both men and women and on their shared origins in the maternal space of the Imaginary. Nowhere in *India Song* is this more apparent than in the startling, to some viewers even shocking, sequence towards the end of the reception when the vice-consul's scream rips through the artificial decorum of the colonial bourgeoisie. The entire sequence lasts for nearly twenty-five minutes and is punctuated by the man shouting that he wants to stay with Anne-Marie Stretter, just for one night, knowing that he will be rejected and expelled from the embassy by the other guests who simply carry on talking as if nothing had happened. But the man's overt display of intense emotions disrupts not only the false politeness of middle-class society, but also the dominant model of masculinity with its insistence on rationality and control. In mainstream cinema, as Chion has pointed out, the scream is normally associated with women or, more rarely, it may function as an expression of virile power, for instance in the Tarzan movies (Chion 1993: 77). The male scream in *India Song*, by contrast, is exceptional in the history of contemporary cinema, since it represents male vulnerability, not dominance (Chion 1993: 78). This powerful expression of desire by a male protagonist breaks down the coherence of language and logic that underpins the Symbolic order and thus reinforces the implicit link between the vice-consul and the 'mad' beggarwoman and perhaps with women in general. Indeed, his screaming, crying and sobbing throughout this part of the film are reminiscent of the 'hysterical' behaviour usually attributed to women and may also remind us of the dying woman's scream in Duras's novel *Moderato cantabile* (1958) or of Lol V. Stein's scream at the end of the ball at S. Tahla. Like the salesman in *Nathalie Granger*, the vice-consul reveals the emotions, passions and vulnerabilities that men are supposed to repress in order to conform to the construct of patriarchal masculinity. But what is particularly disturbing about this sequence in *India Song* is the sense of helplessness that reverberates in the man's voice, like that of an abandoned child screaming for his mother. The scream thus announces the male character's regression to the Imaginary and the maternal, condensed in the theme tune of *India Song* itself. For, as the vice-consul says, 'ma mère jouait *India Song*. Le morceau est là depuis sa mort'.[16] As Royer has remarked, it is significant that the vice-consul shouts out Anne-Marie Stretter's mother's name, Anna-Maria Guardi, and thereby challenges the patriarchal system whose symbolic foundation is, of course, the name-of-the-Father (Royer 1997: 52).

Duras's representations of both her male and her female protagonist, then, clearly highlight her intention of dismantling gender categories. This blurring of the boundaries between 'masculine' and 'feminine' appearance and behaviour is equally implicit in several shots featuring Anne-Marie Stretter accompanied by two or more male figures. The first such image appears early on in the film, when the camera follows Anne-Marie, surrounded by Michael Richardson and the young guest, as they leave the large drawing room inside the embassy and go outside into the park. As we listen to the female off-screen voices talk about the lepers and the beggarwoman, the image-track focuses on the woman and the two men, as they slowly descend the staircase leading to the park (see Plate 3). What is striking about this shot is the rigorous visual equivalence between the men's and the woman's postures and movements, as their synchronised steps remind us of the choreographed, stylised configuration of a ballet. The mirror effect suggested by this shot creates a strong sense of gender indeterminacy and identification between the male and female figures, as Duras undermines the conventional construction of the gendered walk that would contrast the long and energetic 'masculine' stride with the short and dainty steps associated with the 'feminine' gait. The symmetry implicit in this sequence subverts the patriarchal construction of both gender and of heterosexuality which depends on the perception of differences rather than similarities between men and women. Duras's unconventional approach to the filming of the male and female protagonists in *India Song* replaces this heterosexual model with a more gender-ambiguous, bisexual pattern of relationships. The correspondence between gender symmetry and bisexuality is particularly striking in the scene following the vice-consul's first appearance,

16 'my mother used to play *India Song*. The music has been there since her death.'

where we see Anne-Marie Stretter in her black dressing gown, stretched out on the floor, next to Michael Richardson. While in the subsequent medium shot the camera lingers on the woman's breast, the latter is almost level with that of the man whose naked torso erotises the male body in a way that contradicts mainstream film practices. This image, then, presents a clear alternative to the dominant visual codes, according to which only the female body is sexualised and appropriated by the spectator's gaze. The symmetry between the male and the female body in this sequence of *India Song*, by contrast, suggests that either both or neither are sexualised and that, in any case, the spectator's gaze is drawn towards both the man and the woman. In *India Song*, more clearly than in *Nathalie Granger*, Duras constructs a bisexual viewing position which can be taken up by all spectators, regardless of whether they are male or female. As Mayne has remarked, the bisexual undercurrents in films by women directors disrupt the oppositional paradigm of narrative cinema which provided the basis for Mulvey's theory of the male gaze and the role of the woman as erotic spectacle (Mayne 1990: 118). This observation is certainly relevant to our study of Duras who breaks down the hierarchical oppositions underpinning representations of gender in Hollywood cinema. At the same time, Durassian cinema questions the codes of heterosexual pornography which, as Mayne has pointed out, is based on clearly marked divisions between male and female partners who are constructed as sexual subjects and objects, masters and slaves respectively (Mayne 1990: 129). Indeed, contrary to the almost compulsive repetition in mainstream cinema of more or less explicit 'sex scenes', the latter are conspicuously absent from Duras's films. In *India Song* the encounters between Anne-Marie Stretter and the small circle of admirers who surround her express mutual affection rather than the woman's 'possession' by the men. Michael Richardson's gestures of empathy and tenderness towards Anne-Marie Stretter thus suggest a relationship of mutual recognition and understanding which contests dominant constructions of heterosexuality, especially in pornographic cinema. Made in 1975 at a time when, according to Susan Hayward, 50 per cent of French films were pornographic (Hayward 1993: 244), *India Song* represented a notable exception to this tendency. The reason for this lies not just in Duras's refusal to be swept along by any dominant trend, but also in the fact that her entire work is infused with an erotic and sensual flavour that goes beyond representations of the purely sexual. This eroticism sustains and emphasises desire rather than its fulfilment, which is suggested in *India Song* when Delphine Seyrig *nearly* kisses Claude Mann in a long 'take' that is all the more powerful for remaining understated. The almost unbearable tension of this sequence is heightened, furthermore, by the slow, sensual theme tune of *India Song* that accompanies it.

One important aspect of Duras's treatment of sexuality, then, consists in her questioning of both the oppositional constructions of gender and of heterosexuality, since the two are inextricably linked in patriarchal cultures. At the same time, the disruption in *India Song* of these dominant paradigms introduces a certain homoerotic current which might explain the fascination that this film holds for gay audiences (Thélu 1980: 17). A closer analysis of *India Song* shows that the homoerotic aspect of the film can be traced both on the sound-track, through the dialogue between the two female voices, and on the image-track where it is staged primarily in terms of men looking at other men. Although the male gaze is still central to the visual construction of *India Song*, it no longer corresponds to the subject/ object divisions of patriarchal culture. On the contrary, it expresses a relation of proximity to the other, instead of the need for possession and control with which it remains associated in mainstream films. If the latter represent heterosexual desire as stemming from a perceived opposition between the male 'subject' and the female 'object', the homoeroticism that runs through *India Song* is grounded in relations of identification between the male protagonists. As Kaja Silverman has remarked with regard to experimental feminist cinema: 'It is [...] this conjunction of identification and eroticism which I would describe as the "censored, repressed elements of the feminine" and which I believe to have a vital relation to feminism' (Silverman 1988: 151). In *India Song* these 'repressed elements of the feminine', associated with the Imaginary and highlighting relations of similarity and contiguity, appear in a sequence which, at first sight, seems to revolve around the heterosexual couple, but which carries a visual subtext with clear homo-erotic connotations. The sequence in question, which has already been mentioned above, shows Anne-Marie Stretter and Michael Richardson lying next to each other, when a second man enters the room. What immediately strikes the viewer is that, from a distance, this other man looks virtually identical to Michael Richardson, as they are both wearing white trousers and are naked above the waist. These visual similarities between the two male figures evidently suggest a relationship of mutual identification which is further emphasised when the second man sits next to Michael Richardson on the floor. Contrary to conventional representations of the Freudian Oedipal triangle which involves two men vying for the attention of one woman, this sequence creates an unusual sense of closeness between the men, both in terms of their physical resemblances and because of their physical proximity within the frame (see Plate 4). In direct contrast with the Oedipal scenario, the woman is no longer central to the relationship between the men, as she is literally on the edge of the frame, visually 'marginalised' in relation to the mirror image created by the two male figures. This is reinforced by the filming of the male gaze, since the anonymous 'second man' looks directly at Michael Richardson, and not at Anne-Marie Stretter, at the same time as he touches his own breast in an implicitly homoerotic gesture. As in the opening shot of this sequence which focuses on the male and the female protagonist, this scene breaks down patriarchal subject positions, as the distinctions between 'the masculine' and 'the feminine', between heterosexuality and homosexuality begin to disintegrate, both in relation to the figures on screen and to viewers of the film. In *India Song* Duras questions the labelling of individuals and their relationships in terms of rigidly defined categories of gender and sexuality, for as she remarked in an interview with the gay magazine *Le Gai Pied*: 'Il n'y a pas de sexualité masculine ou féminine. Il y a une seule sexualité dans laquelle baignent tous les rapports'[17] (Thélu 1980: 16).

A particularly powerful example in *India Song* of this blending of sexualities comes to light when we look at the underlying correspondences between the film's visual representations of heterosexual relationships, on the one hand, and the homoerotic undertones of the dialogue between the two female voices, on the other. For as the off-screen voices talk about the relationship between Michael Richardson and Anne-Marie Stretter, their evocation of the other couple's love affair alternates and merges with their own. This overlapping of lesbian and heterosexual desire is perhaps most clearly expressed in the play *India Song* which Duras wrote in 1972 at the request of the

17 'There is no masculine or feminine sexuality. There is only one sexuality in which all relationships are steeped.'

director of the National Theatre in London, Peter Hall, and which subsequently became the prototype for the film. The opening remarks of the play specifically draw attention to the anonymous female voices in the following terms: 'Les voix 1 et 2 sont des voix de *femmes*. Ces voix sont jeunes. Elles sont liées entre elles par une histoire d'amour. Quelquefois elles parlent de cet amour, le leur. La plupart du temps elles parlent de l'autre amour, de l'autre histoire. Mais cette autre histoire nous ramène à la leur. De même que la leur, à celle d'India Song'[18] (Duras 1973a: 11). In both the play and the film *India Song*, then, love and desire circulate among the two couples, like a universal energy which is displaced from one protagonist to another. If voice 1 is 'lost' in the story of Anne-Marie Stretter, even to the point of madness, voice 2 'se brûle à sa passion pour la voix 1',[19] since her passion for voice 1 mirrors the latter's obsession with the other woman (Duras 1973a: 11). This constant transference of desire, however, implicates not only Duras's fictional creations, but also the author-director herself, whose lifelong obsession with Anne-Marie Stretter seems to have been transposed on to the female voices of *India Song*. For, as Duras remarked in *La Couleur des mots*, she wrote *Le Ravissement de Lol V. Stein* and *Le Vice consul*, the two fictional predecessors of *India Song*, in the same year, because she felt compelled by a need to exorcise her feelings for Anne-Marie Stretter (Duras and Noguez 1984). In *India Song*, then, the co-presence of sexualities becomes evident from the first shot of Michael Richardson dancing with Anne-Marie Stretter which is accompanied by the dialogue between the two female voices audible on the soundtrack. Their exchange is ambiguous, as voice 2 seems to be expressing both the other couple's feelings for each other and her own love for voice 1 when she says: 'Je vous aime jusqu'à ne plus voir, ne plus entendre, mourir'.[20] Speaking from both the male and the female position, therefore, voice 2 blurs the boundaries of gender as well as any clear-cut definitions of sexuality. A similar ambiguity occurs in a later sequence when the voices talk about the vice-consul's obsession with Anne-Marie Stretter while the

---

18 'The voices 1 and 2 are *women's* voices. These voices are young. They are linked by a love story. Sometimes they talk about this love, theirs. Most of the time they talk about the other love, the other story. But this other story takes us back to theirs. In the same way as theirs takes us back to that of India Song.'

19 'is burning up with her passion for voice 1'

20 'I love you until I can no longer see or hear, until I die.'

camera rests on the man standing in front of the woman's red bicycle. The intense desire implicit in the image is also perceptible in the emotive tone of voice 1 who clearly identifies with the vice-consul as she tells his story of unrequited love. The patterns of identification and desire in *India Song*, therefore, cut across all distinctions in relation to sexual identities. The film evokes a world where sexual desires and energies could be expressed in many different ways, instead of remaining fixed within the existing binary model. This polymorphous quality of *India Song* is underlined in the closing sections where the two female voices from the beginning of the film alternate with the voices of Duras herself and that of Dionys Mascolo, creating an oscillating movement on the soundtrack between the male and the female voice.

In *India Song*, then, Duras continues to dismantle the Symbolic order and question its rigid system of classification which insists on defining and labelling people in terms of their gendered and sexual-ised identities. Instead, the film foregrounds the sense of fluidity and indistinction that is generally associated with the Imaginary. As Royer has pointed out, the predominance of the voice over the image in *India Song* plays a crucial part in this regressive movement towards the Imaginary because of its association with the maternal, 'feminine' energy that remains unrepresentable within the analytical and con-ceptual structures of patriarchal cultures (Royer 1997: 57). This journey back to the mother is suggested by the film's cyclical struc-ture, for if the beggarwoman's exile from the maternal is suggested in the opening sequence, the closing shot of the map traces her return journey to Savannakhet, the place of her origin. However, it is important to stress that in *India Song* the Imaginary is not associated exclusively with women. On the contrary, as in psychoanalytical theory, it appears precisely as the place which precedes the Symbolic order and where biological sex has not yet been aligned with the social constructs of 'masculinity' and 'femininity'. This gender-neutral quality becomes even more prominent in *Agatha* where the privileged use of the disembodied off-screen voices continues to undermine the power of the image and its conventional representations of gender and sexuality.

Agatha

Inspired by Robert Musil's novel *Der Mann ohne Eigenschaften (The Man Without Qualities)* about the incestuous relationship between Ulrich Heimer and his sister Agathe, Duras made *Agatha* in the winter of 1980. The film was released in the following year, at the same time as the play *Agatha*, extracts from which appear at regular intervals within the film. This familiar blend of text and film parallels the equally common conjunction in Duras of autobiography and fiction, as *Agatha* was filmed at the Hôtel des Roches Noires in Trouville on the Normandy coast, where Duras had an apartment. It was also in Trouville that, in the summer of 1980, she met Yann Andréa who was to become her close companion until her death in 1996. Fascinated by her work, the young student from Caen had been writing to Duras virtually every day since he had first seen her at a screening of *India Song*. Moved by the tone of these letters in which she recognised Andréa as a kindred spirit, Duras finally decided to write back and to tell this complete stranger about her life at that time, her terrible loneliness, her depression, her repeated hospitalisation due to alcoholism. When Andréa finally visited her, a bond of mutual recognition and affinity developed immediately, despite the considerable age difference between them, as the 66-year-old Duras fell in love with a man nearly forty years younger than her (Lebelley 1994: 272–9).[21] To add to this potential difficulty, Duras soon discovered that Yann Andréa was gay and that their future relationship would thus remain largely platonic. This lack of sexual fulfilment, together with the unorthodox, even transgressive quality of the relationship, is also reminiscent, of course, of Duras's quasi-incestuous adolescent relationship with her brother Paul. *Agatha* mirrors both relationships, as the film resonates with the off-screen voices of Duras and Andréa who also appears on the image-track where he represents Agatha's anonymous brother.

Following the credit sequence and the by now familiar black screen, the film opens with a shot of an extract from the play *Agatha* announcing the arrival of a man and a woman, both 30 years of age, at a deserted house by the sea. The woman, as we gather from the subsequent narrative, is Agatha who has returned to the house to meet

21 Yann Andréa has given his own, very moving account of his sixteen-year relationship with Duras, see Andréa 1999.

her brother one last time before their final separation. Throughout the remainder of the film, past and present constantly overlap, as brother and sister remember their childhood and adolescent love for each other, while their adult incarnations, in the form of Yann Andréa and Bulle Ogier, drift in and out of the image-track. From an auto-biographical perspective, *Agatha* was Duras's first attempt to recreate and thus begin to come to terms with her relationship with her brother, as is evident from the allusions to 'ce fleuve colonial de notre enfance' (the colonial river of our childhood), when Duras's off-screen voice evokes the villa Agatha which was situated near a river. Like *India Song*, *Agatha* describes the protagonists' regression to the Imaginary domain of childhood and the maternal, as their memories temporarily free them from the constraints of the Symbolic order. This regressive movement in *Agatha* corresponds to the primacy of the voice over the image, as the frequency of the black screen and the initial absence of any physical representation of the protagonists contribute to the sense of disembodiment conveyed by the film. The two Brahms waltzes that alternate with the voices, together with the repeated exterior shots of the sea, the sky and the empty beaches express the longing to return to a childhood whose openness contrasts with the images of enclosed spaces and window frames barring the protagonists' return to this archaic world. From a psychoanalytical point of view, furthermore, the Imaginary signifies the early stages of human experience, outside the patriarchal norms of gendered sexuality, where identification prevails over differentiation. The pre-Symbolic brother/sister relationship in *Agatha* thus evokes the archetypal figure of the twin, as the film narrative insists on the physical and psychological similarities between them. As in *India Song*, Duras uses visual and verbal symmetries to underline the resemblances between the man and the woman. Not only are Agatha's hands said to resemble her brother's, but Duras's off-screen voice also remarks that 'ils ont la même fragilité des yeux, de la peau, la même blancheur'.[22] The central theme of the music also expresses the emotional proximity between the two characters, since the brother agrees to play the Brahms waltz on behalf of Agatha who, following in the footsteps of Nathalie Granger, refuses to learn the piano. Contrary to the hierarchical structures of the Symbolic order, the love between brother

22 'They have the same delicate eyes and skin, the same whiteness.'

and sister in Duras's film is based on a sense of mutual empathy and recognition. This intuitive understanding between them is suggested, for example, when Duras's voice, speaking for Agatha, says: 'J'ai vu que vous pensiez la même chose à me voir que moi de vous avoir vu'.[23] Quite apart from these similarities suggested by the narrative, even the voices of Duras and Andréa resemble each other to such an extent that any perceived differences between the male and the female voice become blurred. The pitch, tone and diction of the two voices are so similar that their origin in terms of the speakers' biological sex is difficult to determine at times, especially during the long sequences in the film where there is no physical representation of the two protagonists.

The pattern of resemblances that underscores the brother/sister relationship is also reflected in the film's visual track, where the recurring images of the open sea suggest the lack of boundaries and distinctions inherent in this relationship. Thus, for instance, when the man evokes his adolescent love for his sister during their seaside holidays, the camera slowly sweeps across the sea in a lateral tracking shot, linking sound and image and reflecting the symbiotic fusional quality of the incestuous relationship. The film's reflexive quality is enhanced, moreover, by its repeated shots of the mirror in the empty lobby of the Hôtel des Roches Noires, creating a parallel with the image of the twins that describes the mysterious affinity between Agatha and her brother. The use of the mirror is particularly striking in the sequence where it reflects and multiplies not only the pillars in the lobby, but also the camera and the cameraman whose blurred, almost liquefied mirror images appear in the background of the frame. The fantasmatic aspect of this shot is heightened, further-more, by the appearance of Bulle Ogier who enters on the left-hand side of the frame and whose multiple reflections are subsequently caught in the mirror as she slowly walks across the entrance hall of the hotel. This sequence transforms the interior location of *Agatha* into a corridor of mirrors and contributes to the hallucinatory quality of the film's images. As Leslie Hill has pointed out, 'it is at times unclear whether these are real images, or simply reflections of images, or indeed reflections of reflections of images' (Hill 1993: 141). The film's infinite mirror structure, amplified by the music echoing

23 'I saw that when you looked at me you were thinking the same thing as I was thinking when I looked at you.'

through the empty hotel, constantly affirms the primacy of identification and similarity, by contrast with the differentiating, oppositional structures of the Symbolic order. The film's association with the Imaginary is perhaps most powerfully condensed in Agatha's memory of her brother playing the piano, as Duras's offscreen voice says: 'Je me voyais dans une glace en train d'écouter mon frère jouer pour moi seule au monde [...] et je me suis vue emportée dans le bonheur de lui ressembler'.[24] The classic Durassian metaphors of the mirror and the music, allied with the pervasive images of the sea, create the film's fluid, boundless quality. Like brother and sister who go beyond social taboos, *Agatha* itself defies all barriers and limitations. The man and the woman in Duras's film both transcend and transgress society's notions of identity, remaining in an undifferentiated childhood world which is reminiscent, in some respects, of the genderless utopia evoked by Wittig in *Les Guérillères* (1969) and in *The Straight Mind and Other Essays* (1992). The film's affinity with this Imaginary universe is intensified by the sad, slow rendition of the Brahms waltz which accompanies the following comment about Agatha and her brother: 'Ils sont restés l'un l'autre dans l'enfance même de leur amour'[25] (Duras 1981: 59). The fact that, at this point, only the words themselves appear on the screen, as the camera moves down a page from the play *Agatha*, suggests here that the protagonists' love is both unrepresentable and unspeakable. The force of their emotions, furthermore, is such that it cannot be enacted, either in a play or a film, as only the graphic representations of extracts from the play seem to guarantee a certain detachment from the intensity of the relationship: 'Toujours la douceur, la voix fêlée, brisée d'un émoi insoutenable, non jouable, non représentable'[26] (Duras 1981: 20).

The themes of both childhood and of forbidden love, closely linked in *Agatha*, run through Duras's entire work, where they are invariably seen in a positive light, as the freedom and spontaneity of desire is contrasted with the repressive connotations of a particular notion of 'adulthood', constructed by the normalising discourses of patriarchal

---

24 'I saw myself in a mirror listening to my brother who was playing only for me, as if I were the only one in the world [...] and I saw myself being carried away by the happiness of resembling him.'

25 'They have both remained in the very childhood of their love.'

26 'Still the gentleness, the cracked voice, broken by an unbearable emotion, unplayable, unrepresentable.'

society. Within the theoretical framework of classical Freudian psychoanalysis, for example, 'adult' sexuality is always defined in terms of
reproductive heterosexuality which prohibits cross-gender identification and which, instead, relies on the categorical differentiation
between men and women. *Agatha*, on the contrary, undercuts this
model through its insistence on the identificatory relationship between brother and sister and through its explicit infringement upon
social norms concerning 'acceptable' expressions of desire. The
marginal position occupied by the couple in relation to the Symbolic
order is implicit in the film narrative itself, as memories of their
summer holidays at the villa Agatha allude to their sense of separateness
from the rest of the family. Indeed, as Agatha's narrative implies, it
was their parents and their other siblings who, one summer, found
out about their incestuous relationship: 'Et des escaliers blanc de la
villa Agatha sont descendus nos jeunes frères et sœurs et nos parents
[...] Tout a été recouvert pour la première fois'.[27] This opposition
between the social order, on the one hand, and the unorthodox couple
of sister and brother, on the other hand, is constructed through their
strong association with the sea as a Durassian symbol of freedom
which tempts both of them to swim out 'au-delà des balises autori-
sées, au-delà de tout'.[28] The transgressive nature of their love, allied
with its prohibition by society, create an implicit correspondence in
the film's thematic structure between incest and homosexuality. In
this respect, it was perhaps not a coincidence that Duras chose the
man whom she herself described as 'Y. A., homosexuel' to play the
role of the brother (Duras 1987: 89). Indeed, the vocabulary used in
the film narrative to refer to the brother/sister relationship strongly
echoes the familiar patriarchal constructions of homosexuality in
terms of guilt, sin and criminality. Thus, the off-screen voice of Yann
Andréa alludes to an anonymous group of people who speak about the
relationship between Agatha and her brother as 'coupable' and
'criminel'. However, it is precisely the transgressive nature of their
desire and the prohibition attached to it that keeps their feelings alive.
As in *Le Navire Night*, the survival of desire itself depends on certain
obstacles, for example the physical distance between the lovers in

27 'And our young brothers and sisters and our parents came down the white
   staircase at the villa Agatha. [...] Everything was covered up for the first time.'
28 'beyond the buoys marking out the [authorised] swimming area, beyond everything'

both films and, more specifically in *Agatha*, the social laws that forbid incest. Paradoxically, the patriarchal law which prohibits their relationship also sustains their desire, nourished by 'cette interdiction qui est notre loi',[29] as the male narrative voice puts it. For Duras, all marginal sexualities define themselves partly by their dissidence from and transgression of social and sexual norms, which she considers to be a vital ingredient of sexual desire itself. For as she remarked in her interview with *Gai Pied*: 'Il n'y a pas de libération des interdits, on le sait quand même, l'interdit est partie intégrante de la sexualité même'[30] (Thélu 1980: 16). The theme of taboo and transgression in *Agatha* is also implicit in the recurring, albeit rather blurred images suggesting the outlines of a forest. In Duras the forest has become a symbol not only of her own encounters with the tropical jungles of her childhood, but also of the wild, uncharted territory of the unconscious, repudiated and repressed by the rational structures of patriarchal cultures. The forest as a symbol of transgression appears in several works by Duras, such as the 1969 text and film *Détruire dit-elle* where it is closely linked to lesbian sexuality and, of course, in *Agatha* where it accompanies the incest motif.

Viewed from the point of view of feminist psychoanalyis, the film's thematic focus on the incestuous couple's infringement of sexual norms might be interpreted in terms of an underlying opposition between the maternal order of the Imaginary and the Symbolic Law-of-the-Father. It is clear that, while the latter prohibits incest as well as other dissident sexualities, Duras's allegiance lies with the former, as her evocation of the brother/sister relationship is devoid of the outrage and condemnation it usually provokes. As Michel Mesnil has remarked: 'Dernier tabou bourgeois, l'inceste n'est nullement vécu comme crime dans *Agatha*'[31] (Mesnil 1981: 151). The implicit link in *Agatha* between the Imaginary and sexual transgression surfaces at several points in the film, where the figure of the mother shows a certain complicity with and understanding of the relationship between her children. The first reference to her seemingly arbitrary presence in the film occurs as, in an extended narrative flashback, Agatha remembers her decision to stop playing the piano, when suddenly the

29 'this prohibition that is our law'
30 'There is no liberation from prohibitions, we do know that prohibitions are an integral part of sexuality itself.'
31 'In *Agatha* incest, the last middle-class taboo, is not at all experienced as a crime.'

mother appears, looking and smiling at the children: 'Elle a regardé ses enfants longtemps avec cette même douceur que prend votre regard parfois'.[32] This triangular relationship between the mother and her two children creates a certain pre-Oedipal structure from which the father is absent. In a biographical context this corresponds, of course, to Duras's own childhood experience where, following her father's death, her mother and her brother Paul came to occupy centre stage. From a psychoanalytical perspective, however, it is evident that the mother in *Agatha* acts as her children's covert ally who tacitly accepts their 'forbidden love' and is thus complicitous with their breaking of the paternal law. Thus, as she listens to their conversations, she suddenly notices their use of the formal 'vous' to speak to each other, but unlike other people, who may think of this unusual form of address between brother and sister as part of a game, the mother understands its significance as a cover for the underlying intimacy between them. And on her deathbed she tells Agatha never to leave her brother: 'Elle a dit ce jour-là: "Mon enfant, ne te sépare jamais de lui, ce frère que je te donne".'[33] The fact that the mother thinks of her son as a symbolic gift to her daughter suggests that, within the framework of the film at least, all three protagonists are situated outside the Symbolic order which depends precisely on the suppression of the earlier relationship between mothers and children and on the exchange of women among men. As in *India Song*, furthermore, Duras creates a strong association in *Agatha* between the figure of the mother and the ever present music. Significantly, given the film's emphasis on the various similarities between Agatha and her brother, it is the mother who points out that her two eldest have the same hands, perfect for playing an instrument. Although music in Duras is always linked to the pre-linguistic world of early childhood, the adult authority and enforced discipline that characterises the piano lesson in her work are clearly manifestations of the Symbolic order which destroys the freedom and spontaneity of the Imaginary. But the mother in *Agatha*, unlike other maternal figures in Duras, refuses to collude with society. Instead, she accepts her daughter's unwillingness to learn the piano and agrees that her son will henceforth play on Agatha's behalf: 'Et puis elle a dit que oui, qu'elle

---

32 'She looked at her children for a long time, with that same gentleness that your gaze sometimes has.'

33 'On that day she said: "My child, don't ever leave the brother I'm giving you".'

acceptait, qu'Agatha était libérée de cette obligation d'apprendre le piano, que c'en était fini'.[34] The love between brother and sister in *Agatha*, then, affirms the archaic mother/child bond, as the affinity between Agatha, the brother and the mother directly contravenes the laws of patriarchal society, which attempts to reassert its authority by forcing the incestuous couple to abide by its norms. Following the discovery of their relationship, they are forced to get married by an anonymous social order, so that 'the scandal' can be swept under the carpet: 'On nous a mariés dans les années d'après. Tout a été recouvert'.[35] The unusual grammatical construction 'they married us' suggests that Agatha and her brother have been deprived of both their subjectivity and their agency, as they take up their position in patriarchal society against their will. The repressive social norms governing the Symbolic order are also suggested in visual terms through the recurring images of a house, presumably the villa Agatha, whose railings and staircases evoke the tangle of barriers and limitations that permanently thwart the central relationship in the film.

The separation between brother and sister is perhaps more ambiguous, however, than it first appears, since the very surival of their desire, as we have seen, depends on the intervention of the Symbolic order which temporarily disconnects them both from the maternal and from each other. But more importantly, as the film narrative repeatedly suggests, the symbiotic tie of the incestuous relationship needs to be loosened, because otherwise brother and sister might be incapable of existing as two separate individuals. This central ambiguity in *Agatha* signals Duras's implicit critique of the two fundamental modes of being and relating in patriarchal societies. At one extreme, the dominant models of gender and sexuality insist on the oppositional construction of 'masculine' and 'feminine' identities which leave little scope for relationships based on mutual recognition and identification. These models, then, emphasise gendered differences at the expense of similarities, perpetuating a society where the notion of 'difference' has always been used to explain and justify inequalities between men and women. At the other extreme, Duras's fictional protagonists often reject the Symbolic order altogether and, instead, remain attached to the Imaginary maternal universe, where

34 'And then she said yes, she agreed that Agatha was freed from this obligation to learn the piano, that it was over.'
35 'They married us in the following years. Everything was covered up.'

sameness prevails over difference. In the case of *Agatha*, however, this position has its own serious disadvantages because, like the spectator who becomes mesmerised by the film's narcissistic fascination with mirrors and echoes, the two protagonists risk drowning in a sea of reflections which threatens to destroy their sense of self.[36] In this context, the significance of the sea as a primary visual symbol becomes ambiguous. For in *Agatha*, as in Duras's other work, the sea represents not only freedom and the dissolution of all boundaries, but also a more sinister destructive power, as Agatha and her brother repeatedly express their fear of being swallowed up by the vast expanse of water: 'C'est une peur identique à la sienne qui est la peur d'Agatha, celle de la mer, celle de son engloutissement dans la mer'.[37] As Michelle Royer has pointed out, this dualistic representation of the sea corresponds to a similarly ambivalent maternal figure who is seen by Duras alternately as a source of nourishment and protection and as an annihilating force (Royer 1997: 91). The image of the sea in *Agatha*, then, evokes both the blissful union between brother and sister as well as the potentially destructive nature of this fusional relationship which seems to be averted by the sister's imminent departure. Throughout the film, the tension between sameness and difference suggests the importance of achieving a certain balance between the two extreme positions, which only seem to allow for either narcissistic mirroring or total separation between the protagonists. As Pascal Bonitzer has observed, this constant oscillation between identification and separation is partly due to the ambiguous status in the film of Bulle Ogier and Yann Andréa who are and yet are not Agatha and her brother (Bonitzer 1981: 55). Indeed, the entire film traces the dialectical movement between togetherness and separateness, childhood and adulthood, closeness and distance, reflected in the alternate use of the familiar 'tu' and the formal 'vous' in the exchanges between brother and sister. Separation and reunion as contrapuntal themes in *Agatha* are also embedded in the film's formal construction, for while the desynchronisation of sound and image reintroduce a familiar sense of discontinuity, the narrative recounted by the off-screen voices corresponds to a larger extent than in previous films to the images

36 For a more detailed discussion of the myth of Narcissus in relation to Durassian cinema, see Royer, 1997: 39–41.

37 'This fear is identical to his, it's Agatha's fear of the sea, of being swallowed up by the sea.'

projected on to the screen. However, given the familiar definitions of the Imaginary as part of the feminine, maternal domain of identifications and resemblances and of the Symbolic as representing the paternal law that introduces separation and difference, it is interesting to note that throughout the film it is Agatha who initiates the process of separation, while her brother pleads with her to delay her departure: 'Retardez-le [le départ] seulement d'un an, je vous en supplie'.[38] This reversal of associations further reinforces Duras's reluctance to accept any fixed gender categories, even those constructed by contemporary feminist theory.

In the three films investigated in this chapter Duras dismantles the patriarchal framework that defines relationships in terms of binary oppositions and mutually exclusive categories. Instead, Durassian cinema breaks down socially constructed identities, as her protagonists can no longer be slotted into clearly delineated models of gender and sexuality. Masculinity and femininity, heterosexuality and homosexuality all become part of the same original expression of libidinal energy. As she remarked in an interview, Duras envisaged a future society that would no longer be based on existing gender divisions, but that would be pervaded by a 'neutral' energy that is neither masculine nor feminine (Lamy 1981: 69). In terms of French feminist theory, this utopian vision seems to endorse the transcendence of identities advocated by Julia Kristeva in her essay 'Women's Time' (see Kristeva 1982) rather than Luce Irigaray's 'culture of difference' (see Irigaray 1993). And yet, despite her resistance to immutable constructs of 'self', in *Agatha* Duras also warns of the dangers inherent in the potential loss of all identity. As the film clearly suggests, the perpetual mirroring between brother and sister threatens to swallow up the differences between them, destroying their very existence as two separate beings. What Duras implicitly advocates through all her films, then, is the importance of going beyond the opposition between sameness and difference itself and to adopt instead a model of relationships where proximity and distance, similarities and differences could co-exist, regardless of sex, gender or sexuality.

38 'Delay it [the departure] by just one year, I beg you.'

References

Andréa, Y. (1999), *Cet amour-là*, Paris, Pauvert.

Bonitzer, P. (1981), 'Agatha et les lectures illimitées', *Cahiers du cinéma*, 329: 55–6.

Butler, J. (1990), *Gender Trouble: Feminism and the Subversion of Identity*, London, Routledge.

Chion, M. (1993), *La Voix au cinéma*, Paris, Seuil.

Duras, M. (1973), *Nathalie Granger, suivi de La Femme du Gange*, Paris, Gallimard.

Duras, M. (1973a), *India Song*, Paris, Gallimard.

Duras, M. (1977), *Le Camion*, Paris, Minuit.

Duras, M. (1981), *Agatha*, Paris, Minuit.

Duras, M. (1987), *La Vie matérielle*, Paris, Gallimard, Folio.

Duras, M. *et al.* (1979), *Marguerite Duras*, Paris, Editions Albatros.

Duras, M. and Gauthier, X. (1974), *Les Parleuses*, Paris, Minuit.

Duras, M. and Noguez, D. (1984), *La Couleur des mots*, interview, BAC.

Hayward, S. (1993), *French National Cinema*, London, Routledge.

Heathcote, O. (2000), 'Excitable silence: the violence of non-violence in *Nathalie Granger*', in Williams, J. (ed.), *Revisioning Duras: Film, Race, Sex*, Liverpool, Liverpool University Press.

Hill, L. (1993), *Marguerite Duras: Apocalyptic Desires*, London, Routledge.

Irigaray, L. (1974), *Speculum, de l'autre femme*, Paris, Minuit.

Irigaray, L. (1977), *Ce sexe qui n'en est pas un*, Paris, Minuit.

Irigaray, L. (1993), *Je, tu, nous: Towards a Culture of Difference*, London, Routledge.

Irigaray, L. (1994), *Thinking the Difference: For a Peaceful Revolution*, London, The Athlone Press.

Kaplan, E. A. (1983), *Women and Film: Both Sides of the Camera*, London, Methuen.

Kaplan, E. A. (1984), 'Is the gaze male?', in Snitow A., Stansell, C. and Thompson, S. (eds.), *Desire: The Politics of Sexuality*, London, Virago.

Kristeva, J. (1982), 'Women's time', in Keohane, N. O. *et al.* (eds), *Feminist Theory: A Critique of Ideology*, Brighton, Harvester Press.

Lamy, S. and Roy, A. (1981), *Marguerite Duras à Montréal*, Montréal, Editions Spirale.

Lebelley, F. (1994), *Duras ou le poids d'une plume*, Paris, Grasset.

Mayne, J. (1990), *The Woman at the Keyhole: Feminism and Women's Cinema*, Bloomington, Indiana University Press.

Mesnil, M. (1981), 'Agatha', *Esprit*, 12: 148–52.

Mulvey, L. (1975), 'Visual Pleasure and Narrative Cinema', *Screen*, 16(3): 198–209.

Oliver, B. (1985), 'Le Thème de la violence de *Moderato cantabile* à *Nathalie Granger*', *Atlantis*, 10(2): 31–44.

Porte, M. (1983), 'The Places of Marguerite Duras', *Enclitic*, 7(2): 55–62.

Royer, M. (1997), *L'Ecran de la passion*, Mount Nebo, Boombana Publications.

Silverman, K. (1988), *The Acoustic Mirror: The Female Voice in Psychoanalysis and Cinema*, Bloomington, Indiana University Press.

Thélu, R. (1980), 'The thing: entretien avec M. Duras', *Le Gai Pied*, 20: 16.

Turkle, S. (1979), *Psychoanalytic Politics: Jacques Lacan and Freud's French Revolution*, London, Burnett Books.

Walsh-Harrington, G. (1999), 'The function of the incidental song in contemporary French and Belgian cinema', Ph.D. thesis, University of Sheffield.

Wittig, M. (1969), *Les Guérillères*, Paris, Minuit.

Wittig, M. (1992), *The Straight Mind and Other Essays*, Hemel Hempstead, Harvester Wheatsheaf.

Afterword

Marguerite Duras was one of the great innovators of twentieth-century cinema and literature. Yet her films, even more so than her novels, have sometimes been criticised for being too abstract and intellectual, accessible only to a select group of initiates. Such criticism is quite unjustified, however, since her work reflects not only the passion and sadness of her personal experience, but also her deep political commitment as a socialist and as a feminist. For Duras, the conventions of mainstream film with its hierarchical divisions and oppositions represented the cinematographic equivalent of social power structures that had to be abolished before a new, more egalitarian society and culture could emerge. The films of Duras are necessarily experimental and innovatory, since she attempted to create new forms of expression and a different experience for her spectators by replacing the obsessive focus in Western cultures on the explicit and the visible with a cinema that privileges words, sounds and the imagination. Her work both in literature and in film distinguishes itself by its oblique, elusive quality which evokes her protagonists' inner landscape instead of dwelling on the appearances of the external world. But in addition to this intriguing mixture of the personal and the political, the compelling nature of Durassian cinema lies in its aesthetic creativity and its characteristic orchestration of music, images and voices. Ironically, however, the name of Duras became widely known to international cinema audiences, not through her own films, but through the 1992 adaptation of her novel *L'Amant*. Directed by Jean-Jacques Annaud, whose previous films *Le Nom de la rose (The Name of the Rose)* (1986) and *L'Ours (The Bear)* (1989) had already been very popular, *The Lover* became an instant box-office hit. But in spite of the film's success, the disparity between mainstream cinema and the work of Duras was exemplified by Annaud's highly commercialised adaptation and the ensuing confrontation between the two directors and their contrasting styles.

Although in 1987 Duras had agreed to a request by producer Claude Berri to work on the film with Annaud, serious health problems in the late 1980s prevented her from doing so. In 1989, when the two directors first met, Duras had been in hospital for eight months, and was thus unable to participate in the writing of the screenplay which was produced instead by Annaud and Gérard Brach. For Duras, however, neither the screenplay nor the multi-million dollar film production were appropriate to her autobiographical novel *L'Amant*. A long and acrimonious dispute followed, until Duras who had advised Annaud on the making of the film, was eclipsed altogether from the proceedings. In her typically indomitable fashion, however, she decided to write her own version of the screenplay which was published as *L'Amant de la Chine du Nord* in June 1991. A close reading of Annaud's *The Lover* shows that several key scenes in the film, such as the young Duras's journey from Sadec to Saigon in the Chinese lover's black limousine, were informed by descriptions included in the 1991 text and not in the original 1984 novel on which the film was supposedly based. It would appear, therefore, that despite her ongoing quarrel with Annaud at that time, important sections of Duras's revised text were nevertheless incorporated into the film.

A brief comparison between *The Lover* and Duras's own idiosyncratic approach to cinema highlights the reasons for the disagreement between the two directors. Filmed entirely on location in Vietnam, *The Lover* focuses primarily on the visual representation of external details and reflects Annaud's concern with the accuracy of certain 'facts' mentioned in *L'Amant*. Although the film has an authentic flavour, due to its realism and local colour, it entirely lacks the evocative power of Durassian cinema. For Duras herself never tried to provide precise and 'truthful' descriptions of people and places, because the subjective nature of memory and perception makes such attempts at 'objectivity' a futile enterprise. Thus, it is impossible to expect *L'Amant*, written fifty-five years after the events described, to be a 'realistic' fictional portrayal of Duras's childhood and adolescence. What she aimed to convey both in the book and in what might have been her own film version of it was her emotional experience of her life in Vietnam, her painful relationship with her mother, her love affair with the Chinese man, and not whether her shoes were gold or black. Indeed, judging by her own filmmaking practices, it was unnecessary to go to Vietnam to make *The Lover*, since her own films about Calcutta, Venice or Rome were all shot on low budgets in or near Paris. Moreover, because Annaud read *L'Amant* as the author's 'life story', *The Lover* is constructed like a linear autobiographical narrative and thus fails to account for the difficulties and ambiguities surrounding the young Duras's search for identity which is a central preoccupation in the 1984 novel. Instead, the multiple perspectives and voices that run through the written text are replaced in *The Lover* by the obsessive focus on the physical appearance of Jane March, the 17-year-old English girl chosen by Annaud to play the role of the young Duras. While Annaud's film presumably owes its popularity partly to the fact that it conforms to the dominant codes of representation, it undermines the cinematographic writing of Duras's own films and their emphasis on verbal and vocal as well as visual forms of expression.

Both the blurb on the cover of the English translation of *L'Amant* and Annaud's film created the mistaken assumption that the book belonged to a certain well-worn tradition of female-authored, semipornographic novels. Although the film does attempt to convey the desire and sexual passion evoked in the novel, the explicit and monotonously recurring sex scenes confirm the sensationalism which surrounded the launch of the book outside France. *The Lover* was undoubtedly a great commercial success, which did not do justice, however, to either of the two texts by Duras on which it was modelled. Its loud realism and its insistence on reaffirming the power of the image, moreover, are the antithesis of the subtle, understated poetry that is the hallmark of Durassian cinema. Unfortunately, her dream of making her own film about the events she described in *L'Amant* remained unfulfilled when she died in March 1996. Her other films, however, have retained their magical timeless quality as the breathtaking beauty of the images in *Aurélia Steiner (Melbourne)* or in *Le Navire Night* merge with the haunting echoes of her voices and her music to create an unusually powerful viewing experience.

Filmography

La Musica (1966) 80 mins, b/w

Co-directed with Paul Seban
Production company: les Films Raoul Ploquin
Screenplay: Marguerite Duras
Photography: Sacha Vierny
Sound: Guy Villette
Music: Schubert
Editing: Eric Pluet
Actors: Delphine Seyrig (the woman), Julie Dassin (the young girl), Robert
    Hossein (the man)

Détruire, dit-elle (1969) 90 mins, b/w

Production company: Ancinex, Madeleine Films
Screenplay: Marguerite Duras
Photography: Jean Penzer
Sound: Luc Berini
Editing: Henri Colpi
Actors: Nicole Hiss (Alissa), Catherine Sellers (Elisabeth Alione), Michael
    Lonsdale (Stein), Henri Garcin (Max Thor), Daniel Gélin (Bernard Alione)

Jaune le soleil (1971) 80 mins, b/w

Production company: Albina Films
Screenplay: Marguerite Duras
Photography: Ricardo Aronovitch
Sound: Luc Berini
Editing: Suzanne Baron
Actors: Catherine Sellers, Sami Frey, Dionys Mascolo, Diurka, Michael
    Lonsdale

Nathalie Granger (1972) 83 mins, b/w

Production company: Luc Moullet et Cie
Screenplay: Marguerite Duras
Photography: Ghislain Cloquet
Sound: Paul Lainé, Michel Vionnet, Michèle Muller
Music: Czerny
Editing: Nicole Lubtchansky
Actors: Lucia Bose (Isabelle Granger), Jeanne Moreau (the friend), Valérie
    Mascolo (Nathalie Granger), Nathalie Bourgeois (Laurence Granger),
    Gérard Depardieu (the salesman), Dionys Mascolo (Mr Granger), Luce
    Garcia-Ville (the headmistress)

La Femme du Gange (1973) 90 mins, col.

Production company: ORTF
Screenplay: Marguerite Duras
Photography: Bruno Nuytten, Jean Mascolo
Sound: Alain Muslin
Music: Carlos d'Alessio
Editing: Solange Leprince
Principal actors: Catherine Sellers (the woman in black), Nicole Hiss (the
    girl from S. Tahla), Gérard Depardieu (the man on the beach), Dionys
    Mascolo (the traveller), Robert Bonneau (the man at the *casino municipal*)

India Song (1975) 120 mins, col.

Production company: Sunchild, les Films Armorial
Screenplay: Marguerite Duras
Photography: Bruno Nuytten, Jean Mascolo
Sound: Michel Vionnet
Music: Carlos d'Alessio, Beethoven
Editing: Solange Leprince
Actors: Delphine Seyrig (Anne-Marie Stretter), Michael Lonsdale (the Vice-
    Consul), Claude Mann (Michael Richardson), Didier Flamand (the
    young guest), Mathieu Carrière (the young attaché), Vernon Dobtcheff
    (George Crawn)

Son nom de Venise dans Calcutta désert (1976) 118 mins, col.

Production company: Cinéma 9, PIPA, Editions Albatros
Screenplay: Marguerite Duras
Photography: Bruno Nuytten, Jean Mascolo
Sound: Michel Vionnet
Music: Carlos d'Alessio, Beethoven
Editing: Geneviève Dufour

With the participation of Delphine Seyrig, Nicole Hiss, Marie-Pierre Thiébault and Sylvie Nuytten

Des journées entières dans les arbres (1976) 95 mins, col.

Production company: Films A2, SFP Cinéma
Screenplay: Marguerite Duras
Photography: Nestor Almendros
Sound: Jean Millet, Michel Guiffan
Music: Carlos d'Alessio
Editing: Michel Latouche
Actors: Madeleine Renaud (the mother), Bulle Ogier (Marcelle), Jean-Pierre Aumont (the son), Yves Gasq (the barman)

Baxter, Vera Baxter (1976) 90 mins, col.

Production company: Sunchild Production, INA
Screenplay: Marguerite Duras
Photography: Sacha Vierny
Sound: Guillaume Sciama
Music: Carlos d'Alessio
Editing: Dominique Auvray
Actors: Claudine Gabay (Vera Baxter), Delphine Seyrig (the stranger), Gérard Depardieu (Michel Cayre), Noëlle Chatelet (the friend), Claude Anfort (the barman), Nathalie Nell (the mistress)

Le Camion (1977) 80 mins, col.

Production company: Cinéma 9, Auditel
Screenplay: Marguerite Duras
Photography: Bruno Nuytten
Sound: Michel Vionnet
Music: Beethoven
Editing: Dominique Auvray, Caroline Camus
Actors: Marguerite Duras (the woman), Gérard Depardieu (the man)

Le Navire Night (1979) 94 mins, col.

Production company: MK2, Films du Losange
Screenplay: Marguerite Duras
Photography: Pierre Lhomme
Sound: Michel Vionnet
Music: Carlos d'Alessio, Amy Flamer
Editing: Dominique Auvray
Voices: Marguerite Duras and Benoît Jacquot
Actors: Bulle Ogier, Dominique Sanda, Mathieu Carrière

Césarée (1979) 11 mins, col.

Production company: Films du Losange
Screenplay: Marguerite Duras
Photography: Pierre Lhomme
Sound: Michel Vionnet
Music: Amy Flamer
Editing: Geneviève Dufour
Voice: Marguerite Duras

Les Mains négatives (1979) 18 mins, col.

Production company: Films du Losange
Screenplay: Marguerite Duras
Photography: Pierre Lhomme
Sound: Michel Vionnet
Music: Amy Flamer
Editing: Geneviève Dufour
Voice: Marguerite Duras

Aurélia Steiner (Melbourne) (1979) 35 mins, col.

Production company: Paris Audiovisuel
Screenplay: Marguerite Duras
Photography: Pierre Lhomme
Sound: Michel Vionnet
Editing: Geneviève Dufour
Voice: Marguerite Duras

Aurélia Steiner (Vancouver) (1979) 50 mins, b/w

Production company: Films du Losange
Screenplay: Marguerite Duras
Photography: Pierre Lhomme
Sound: Michel Vionnet
Editing: Geneviève Dufour
Voice: Marguerite Duras

Agatha et les lectures illimitées (1981) 90 mins, col.

Production company: Berthemont, INA, Des femmes filment
Screenplay: Marguerite Duras
Photography: Dominique Lerigoleur, Jean-Pierre Meurisse
Sound: Michel Vionnet
Music: Brahms
Editing: Françoise Belleville
Voices: Marguerite Duras and Yann Andréa
Actors: Bulle Ogier and Yann Andréa

L'Homme atlantique (1981) 42 mins, col.

Production company: Berthemont, INA, Des femmes filment
Screenplay: Marguerite Duras
Photography: Dominique Lerigoleur, Jean-Pierre Meurisse
Sound: Michel Vionnet
Music: Brahms
Editing: Françoise Belleville
Voice: Marguerite Duras
Actor: Yann Andréa

Dialogo di Roma (1982) 62 mins, col.

Production company: Lunga Gittata R.A.I.
Screenplay: Marguerite Duras
French voice: Marguerite Duras

Les Enfants (1985) 94 mins, col.

Production company: Berthemont
Screenplay: Marguerite Duras, Jean Mascolo, Jean-Marc Turine
Photography: Bruno Nuytten
Sound: Michel Vionnet
Music: Carlos d'Alessio
Editing: Françoise Belleville
Actors: Alexander Bougosslavsky (Ernesto), Daniel Gélin (Enrico), Tatiana
    Moukhine (Natasha), Martine Chevalier (Nicole), André Dussollier
    (the headmaster), Pierre Arditi (the journalist)

Select bibliography

See also the references sections at the end of each chapter

Bernheim, N. L., *Marguerite Duras tourne un film*, Paris, Albatros, collection ça cinéma, 1975. A fascinating series of interviews about the making of *India Song*, with Duras, the actors and the entire film crew. The book shows the importance of team work in the making of Duras's films and includes excellent photographs by Erica Lennard.

Borgomano, M., *L'Ecriture Filmique de Marguerite Duras*, Paris, Albatros, collection ça cinéma, 1985. An essential book on the cinema of Duras, which provides lucid and detailed readings of her major films. It also contains a useful section on adaptations of Duras's novels by other directors as well as on screenplays written by Duras. The study focuses on Duras's characteristic "cinematographic writing' and on the relationship between her films and her literary work.

Duras, M. and Gauthier, X., *Les Parleuses*, Paris, Minuit, 1974. A series of conversations between Marguerite Duras and Xavière Gauthier about writing, cinema and politics. The book includes discussions about Duras's early films, in particular *Nathalie Granger* and *La Femme du Gange* as well as some interesting autobiographical details and comments about Duras's involvement with feminism and communism.

Duras, M. *et al.*, *Marguerite Duras*, Paris, Albatros, collection ça cinéma, 1979. An excellent collection of interviews and essays, especially informative in relation to *India Song, Son nom de Venise dans Calcutta désert* and *Le Camion*. Reprinted in this book is the famous essay by Jacques Lacan on *Le Ravissement de Lol V. Stein*.

Hill, L., *Marguerite Duras: Apocalyptic Desires*, London, Routledge, 1993. Probably the most comprehensive study in English of Duras's literary texts and films. The book investigates the work of Duras in the context of contemporary critical theory and includes two chapters that focus specifically on her cinema, providing excellent close readings of major films, including *India Song*, *Agatha* and *L'Homme Atlantique*. It also provides an extensive bibliography, including a list of interviews, newspaper articles, radio broadcasts and television appearances by Duras.

Royer, M., *L'Ecran de la passion: une'étude du cinéma de Marguerite Duras*, Mount Nebo, Boombana Publications, 1997. A sophisticated and intricate study centred around the parallels between key themes in Duras's literary texts and the technical innovations of her cinema. The study of the films is set within a conceptual framework informed by literary theory, film theory, feminism and psychoanalysis.

Index

Note: 'n.' after a page reference indicates the number of a note on that page